Ferguson

STYLE AND STYLISTICS

Style and Stylistics

AN ANALYTICAL BIBLIOGRAPHY

Louis T. Milic
Columbia University

New York: THE FREE PRESS
London: COLLIER-MACMILLAN LIMITED

 Collier-Macmillan Canada, Ltd., Toronto, Ontario. Library of Congress Catalog Card Number: 67-19233.

First Printing

CONTENTS

STYLE AND STYLISTICS

INTRODUCTION

1. General

The present Bibliography grew out of a list that I originally compiled for my students in a graduate course in stylistics. The list, under the title *Stylistics: A Preliminary Bibliography,* was requested by a good many scholars and students at other institutions as well. I have now enlarged, revised, and improved the original. In its present form, I believe it is a proper guide to the field of style and stylistics for all who may have an interest in the individual use of language and in the study of that use.

Mainly as a result of the development of linguistics, the study of style has come to interest a great many of late. Much has been published about style and related subjects, some of it in remote and unlikely locations. The study of style is no longer the exclusive domain of the literary critic. The student of stylistics must not be surprised to find himself venturing beyond literary criticism, into aesthetics, linguistic philosophy, logic, epistemology, personality theory, the psychology of perception and learning, linguistic pathology, mathematical linguistics, statistics, computer technology, sociology and anthropology, not to mention the branches of linguistics itself: semantics, grammar, and phonology. I hope that this Bibliography, both in its contents and its arrangement, will provide useful guidance to those who wish to know what the study of style has been in the past and what it is today.

The Bibliography is "analytical" in the sense that it does not merely list titles but, by a system of arrangement, description, and indexing, tries to provide the maximum of useful help to the seeker. It may be forgiven me if I mention here that the over 800 items listed herein were selected from a much larger number that I examined.

2. *Inclusiveness*

This Bibliography makes no claim to completeness, but it is necessary to specify the limits of its coverage. The works listed are all somehow connected with the study of style, some distantly, many very closely. They are predominantly in English and about English literature and language, though works in French and about French literature and language make up a sizable fraction. There are also some items in German and Italian. I feel confident that nearly everything of first importance has been included, especially in the theoretical and methodological sections. In the treatment of particular authors and styles, selectivity has been the informing principle. There also I feel sure that I have neglected very few of the important discussions. I have tried to give a representative selection of the others. Among the thousands of studies of individual authors, I have tried to represent variety in approach, in intention, and in quality.

3. *Starring System*

To insure that attention will be directed to those works that a person new to the field might find it useful to read first, a system of starring has been adopted. An asterisk before an item number should be understood to mean that the work so marked has a claim to prior attention, because it is basic, simple, or introductory, because it constitutes a survey of the current situation, or because it is a major piece of work. The omission of a star, however, should not be taken to mean that such an item is in any way inferior: it simply means that the work is not recommended for introductory study.

4. *Five Parts*

The over 800 items have been classified into five categories and listed chronologically within each part. Part I, Theoretical (Items 1–158), consists of statements and discussions touching the theory of rhetoric and style from Plato to the present. Part II, Methodological (159–300), lists works whose main concern is the problem of how the study of style is to be pursued. Part III, Applied (301–645), is necessarily the largest and the most selective. It includes studies of particular authors, styles, periods and devices, inventories of the stylistic resources of various languages, contrasts between languages, and problems of translation. It has not always been easy to decide whether a given work properly belonged in Part I, II, or III. The decision was based on my estimate of its main intention or effect. Whenever a work contains significant matter belonging to another Part, the other topics are cross-referenced with descriptors. Thus, a theoretical work containing methodological material will be listed in Part I, with a descriptor reading / Method /. (*See* Section 5.)

The last two sections of the Bibliography list sources of information rather than studies. Part IV, Bibliographies (646–682), lists bibliographical aids in two subdivisions: separate bibliographies and bibliographies that are part of other works. Part V, Omnibus (683–730), lists works containing variety of subject matter (Reference) or of authorship (Collections). The collections include some items whose individual contents were not judged entirely relevant for separate listing in Parts I–III but which it was considered worthwhile to list somewhere. They also include a number of books that reprint items listed separately, and which might therefore be useful as texts or readings for courses.

5. *Entry Format*

A typical entry consists of eight bits of information. The following example will illustrate:

*372. 1934 DOBREE, Bonamy, *Modern Prose Style,* 2d. ed., Oxford, 1964
◈
Sel., Paul C. Wermuth, *Modern Essays on Writing and Style,* New York, 1964, pp. 140–154

English prose, 20C / Personality / Types / Modern prose

(a) *The item number,* possibly preceded by an asterisk (*see* Section 3). Within the five Parts of the Bibliography, item numbers represent a chronological listing. Thus Item 372 is in Part III, which runs from 301 to 645. Any work in Part III with a number lower than 372 must have been originally published earlier and any number higher than 372 must be later, with the most recent works all clustered just before 645.

(b) *The year of original publication* when it is known. Otherwise, the year given is that of book publication.

(c) *The name of the author or authors.* Publications like the proceedings of a conference are usually listed by title. Within a given year, listing is alphabetical by author. Thus DOBREE follows BATESON under the year 1934.

(d) *The title of the book or article and periodical.*

(e) *The facts of publication:* place and date. Because of the instability of publishers' firm names owing to the constant merging of publishing houses, I have decided to omit this type of information. In any case, the information is only of value for the purpose of buying books and can easily be obtained elsewhere. Whenever possible, recent reprints of early and out-of-print works are given under facts of publication. This is the case for DOBREE.

(f) *Subsequent appearances.* When all or part of a work is available in a well-known, convenient, or available collection, this information is provided, as it is here (◈). The abbreviation *Repr.* means the work is reprinted in its entirety in the collection; *Sel.,* as in this case, means that a selection from the work appears in the collection. In either case, the precise page numbers of the reprint are given. Though the item may have been frequently reprinted, only one collection is cited. The collection itself is listed in the Bibliography (Part V-B), in this case No. 722, where information as to its other contents is provided.

(g) *Reference to other items.* When a work listed is directly related to another listed work, items are cross-referenced.

(h) *Descriptors:* an indication of the contents of the item. (*See* Section 6).

6. Descriptors

Instead of an ordinary type of annotation to decribe the contents of each item, in the form of one or more sentences, a series of *descriptors* separated by slashes has been given. A descriptor is a word or phrase representing a topic covered by the work. As many topics as are significantly represented in each work have been listed. Descriptors have the advantage that they save space because no words are wasted on the necessary framework of an annotative sentence, which is of necessity highly redundant. Thus, the four descriptors that follow the listing of No. 372 might have to be rendered in a traditional annotation by a sentence something like the following: "This book discusses the style of English prose writers of the twentieth century, stresses the relation between the writer's style and his personality, considers various types and kinds of style and tries to define the concept of modern prose." Such a sentence, of course, is more explicit than a series of descriptors like "English prose, 20C / Personality / Types / Modern prose," but it really gives no more information and takes three times as much space. The descriptor system requires a certain acquaintance with the central concepts of stylistic theory, but that is easily acquired (*see* Section 8).

The descriptors are usually given in order of importance, though in the case of the items in Part III a different formula has been followed. Item 506 furnishes a convenient illustration:

506. 1956 BARISH, Jonas A., "The Prose Style of John Lyly," *English Literary History,* XXIII (1956), 14–35

English prose, 16C / Lyly / Euphuism / Antithesis / Paradox

The first descriptor characterizes the nation with which the work is concerned (England), the type of writing (prose, as opposed to fiction, drama, or poetry), and the period of time

(16th Cent.). The next one tells us that Lyly is the main writer studied, the third that Euphuism is considered, and the next two that antithesis and paradox are significant aspects. We do not learn from the descriptors whether Barish has a significant new thesis nor whether he approves of Lyly or believes that antithesis and paradox are true features of Euphuism. At a certain point, the bibliographer must send the scholar to the work itself. I am satisfied that the descriptors are a convenient and visually rapid way to discover the contents of the works on this list. Moreover, the descriptors provide the basis for Index 3, where the information has been reorganized.

In Part IV, the first descriptor classifies the bibliographical item according to two criteria: the order of its contents, and the amount of commentary it provides. The order may be alphabetical, chronological, or topical; or it may be a combination, say topical with a chronological or alphabetical listing under each topic. The commentary may be evaluative (called "critical"), or it may be merely a descriptive note on the contents ("annotated"); if there is none, the term *list* is used.

7. Indexes

Although the items listed in the Bibliography are roughly classified by the five-part division, additional means of searching have been provided, in the form of three Indexes.

Indexes refer to Item Number, not to page number

Index 1 gives the names of the authors whose works are listed in the Bibliography. It is a finding-list of writers about style.

Index 2 lists the names of writers whose style or whose ideas about style are discussed in the works listed. Authors in Index 2 are the subject matter for the writers in Index 1.

Some writers, however, are listed in both indexes. They are theorists (like Croce or Spitzer), whose ideas have been commented on by other theorists; or they are literary artists (like Proust) whose ideas about style have given them status as critics as well as novelists. Item numbers of books devoted entirely to one author are printed in bold type.

Index 3 is a general index of subjects or topics. It is where the reader will look when he wishes to find out what has been said, for example, about imagery or contrastive study. The Index has been organized into large basic categories, under which are brought together a number of related items, whose relatedness might otherwise escape the user. Thus, there are main headings for American, English, and French literature, with subdivisions for genre, periods, and other topics. The authors belonging to these literatures have been listed together under these headings for convenience but the reference numbers are listed under their individual names in Index 2. There are also main headings for Attribution, Authorship, Figurative language, Linguistics, Methods, Poetics, Psychology, Rhetoric, Semantics, Theory of style, Translation, Types and qualities of style, and Vocabulary. There is no entry under Style proper for the obvious reason that everything could have been placed under such a heading. These main divisions represent, therefore, the principal parts of stylistics. A number of topics that could not usefully be fitted into any heading have been listed separately. Extensive cross-references direct the user to the appropriate main heading.

8. *Definitions of Key Terms*

The names of main headings as well as a number of other terms in stylistics may not be fully understood by all users of this Bibliography. Therefore, the following definitions of headings are offered, not as a contribution to the field, but merely as a road-map for the user:

AFFECTIVE COMPONENT. According to one simplified dualistic model of language, style is the affective or emotive component, as opposed to the cognitive component or meaning; *see also* FORM-CONTENT.

ALTERATION. A writer's modification of his own style.

ARS DICENDI. Any work containing instruction on how to write or speak.

ATTRIBUTION. Attempt to specify the author of an anonymous or uncertainly-credited work.

CONSCIOUSNESS. The deliberate, voluntary component in the stylistic choices made by the writer; i.e., the way he writes because he thinks it beautiful or effective.

CONTEXT. A linguistic or human environment that can influence the stylistic or semantic value of a term, construction, or device.

CONTRASTIVE STUDY. The parallel examination of the stylistic resources of two or more different languages.

CORRECTNESS. A standard of usage in vocabulary and syntax which often reflects artificial educational or social norms.

DETERIORATION. The tendency of CORRECTNESS or of the stylistic resources of a language to change with time, as a result of social change, altered educational standards or the like.

DEVELOPMENT. Chronological change in a writer's style.

DEVIATION. Idiosyncratic movement of an author from the linguistic norm of his time, either by error or innovation.

FOREGROUNDING. Process of suddenly giving prominence to a stylistic device by abruptly detaching it from its context; foregrounding depends for its effect on the high predictability (REDUNDANCY) of a uniform background.

FORMATION. The conscious attempt of an author to develop his style, by imitation, precept or other means.

FORM-CONTENT. A distinction deriving from an ancient dualism between what is said and how it is said; in the form "style is the dress of thoughts" (Chesterfield), it is often found inadequate; but in some form it nonetheless underlies every effort to study style; *see also* ORGANIC THEORY; ORNATE FORM.

GRAMMATICALITY. The quality of being in accord with the rules of a grammar; the problem of grammaticality is raised when literary artists innovate by violating grammatical propriety.

IDEAL. The belief in the value of a certain quality of style prevalent during a certain period, as "informality and clarity were ideals of style in the reign of Queen Anne"; it should be carefully noted that ideals of style often bear little relationship to the practice of the writers of an era.

IMPRESSIONISM. A traditional approach to style consisting primarily of describing one's own response to a writer's style, sometimes in language suggesting objective description.

INFLUENCE. The impact of some factor on the language or style of a person, group, etc. . . ; e.g., "Aristocratic influence" is the supposed influence of the British aristocracy on the language of the Restoration writers.

INNOVATION. The use of new vocabulary or new grammatical forms.

INTERNAL EVIDENCE. Evidence for ATTRIBUTION based on characteristics of style rather than on biographical events.

INVENTORY. A census of the available choices that a language provides, which constitute the stylistic resources of the language.

LEVELS. In ancient rhetorical theory, the three kinds or "genera" of language, each appropriate to a particular literary purpose, each consisting of a suitable vocabulary and grammar.

MACHINE TRANSLATION. Translation from one language to another by means of programs executed by electronic data-processing machines (computers).

METHODS OR APPROACHES. Ways of pursuing the criticism or description of style; e.g., the linguistic approach, quantitative methods.

MULTIPLE STYLES. *See* PERSONA

NORM. The theoretical average use of a language at a given time; the linguistic norm is an undefinable but useful abstraction; it is easier to recognize DEVIATION from the norm than to define the norm itself.

ORGANIC THEORY. Generally credited to Benedetto Croce, its most distinguished exponent, according to whose view the form and the content coexist and cannot be separated; consequently holders of this view disapprove of the study of style and of rhetoric; *see also* ORNATE FORM.

ORNATE FORM. The derisive name given by Croce to the form-content dualism, the rhetorical theory of style.

PERSONA. The mask a writer assumes when he writes under another identity. The persona theory postulates that a writer is capable of multiple types, depending on the mask or persona he assumes.

PERSONALITY. The prevalent theory that personality is the force that determines the form of a writer's style.

PROSE. Always used for non-fictional prose when it follows a national adjective (e.g., English); otherwise, it may include fiction.

PROSE-VERSE. The problem of defining the nature of the difference and the relationship between prose and verse.

PURISM. A strenuous effort to halt DETERIORATION by imposing unusually stringent standards of CORRECTNESS, usually according to some national formula; *see* SAXONISM.

QUALITIES. Abstract characteristics attributed to a style; e.g., formality, clarity.

QUANTITATIVE METHODS. Objective description of style using observed quantities gathered manually or by computer and ranging from the simple enumerative to the statistical.

REDUNDANCY. In information theory, the tendency of a code to safeguard a message by duplicating features of the signaling-system; word-order and case-forms are aspects of redundancy in English; to be distinguished from the rhetorical term, which signifies pleonasm.

REFLECTION THEORY. Name given to the belief that the style of a man reflects his personality; more often, the view that the style of a period reflects the philosophical and religious views, even the difficulties, of the society; often applied to metaphysical poetry; *see also* PERSONALITY.

REFORM. Sporadic or systematic efforts to arrest DETERIORATION or to produce improvement in the style of a nation during a certain period, or of a group within the nation; e.g., the reform of pulpit style during the Restoration.

SAXONISM. A form of PURISM, advocating the ejection from the English vocabulary of words acquired after the Late Middle English period, notably words of Latin, French, and Greek origin, and the cherishing of words of Germanic origin.

SERIATION. A rhetorical device consisting of a series, or list, of items, usually in random order and exceeding the usual dimensions of copiousness characteristic of balanced prose; much practiced by Rabelais, Swift, and Henry Miller.

STYLISTIC FUNCTION OR STYLISTIC SIGN. The peculiarly stylistic, rather than linguistic, value of a term, construction, or device; according to some theorists, the stylistic function is always different for any given linguistic unit because of the shifting circumstances of the stylistic context.

STYLIZATION. The introduction of a considerable affective

component into a statement; change from plain or neutral style into affective style; *see* AFFECTIVE COMPONENT.

TYPES. Adjectival names given to impressionistic descriptions of style; names like "lucid style," "Ciceronian style," "pulpit style" contain varying but low amounts of verifiable statement; least verifiable seem to be statements describing the style of an entire period.

TYPE-TOKEN RATIO. The ratio of different units to total units (e.g., vocabulary vs. total words of a sample).

TYPOLOGY. Theory or practice of describing the style of a period, a nation, or other group of writers, on the questionable supposition that they have more in common than merely the language they use.

UNCONSCIOUSNESS. The habitual, involuntary component of an author's stylistic choices; i.e., the way he cannot help writing.

VALUE. A distinction based on the presence or absence of style; in this model, good writers have an absolute quality called "style," which bad writers lack.

VIR BONUS. The Platonic notion, conceived as an attack on the Sophists, that effective rhetoric cannot be learned as a separate skill; rhetoric can only derive from the general ability of an ethical man (*vir bonus*), whose goodness is reflected in all kinds of abilities, including the rhetorical.

WORD-CLASS. Part of speech or function-word class.

9. Conclusion

Titles which were added after the consecutive numeration (1–730) had been established have been intercalated in their appropriate chronological places in the Bibliography by means of lower-case letters joined to the preceding item number, thus, 631a comes between 631 and 632. Such added items appear in Indexes 1 and 2 but not in Index 3.

Additional titles have been incorporated into an Appendix at the end. These items are not included in the Index. Notice of errors and omissions which are observed by users of this Bibliography would be welcomed by the compiler at the address given below. In addition, I should be especially thankful for offprints and reprints of items appropriate for inclusion in any further editions. Suggestions about the usefulness of the arrangement would also be well received.

I thank the many scholars who have given me help, suggestions, and copies of their works; the librarians of Columbia University who have been as helpful as they could; Miss Arlene Meurer and Miss Shirley Wiseman, who typed the whole of the previous edition with great good-will; and Mrs. Elizabeth MacAndrew, who not only typed and proofread the entire manuscript but offered such aid and cooperation as almost amounted to collaboration.

Louis T. Milic
Teachers College
Columbia University
New York, New York 10027

Part One

THEORETICAL

*1. c.365 BC PLATO, *Phaedrus,* tr. Harold North Fowler (Loeb Classical Library), London, 1914
◈
Repr., Dudley Bailey, *Essays on Rhetoric,* New York, 1965, pp. 3–54
Rhetoric / Sophistry / Vir bonus / Writing-speech

*2. c.330 BC ARISTOTLE, *Rhetoric,* tr. John Henry Freese (Loeb Classical Library), London, 1926
◈
Sel., Dudley Bailey, *Essays on Rhetoric,* New York, 1965, pp. 55–83
Ars dicendi / Rhetoric, Classical

3. c.325 BC ARISTOTLE, *Poetics,* tr. W. Hamilton Fyfe (Loeb Classical Library), London, 1927
Diction / Metaphor / Sounds / Grammar

*4. c.86 BC *Rhetorica ad Herennium,* tr. Harry Caplan (Loeb Classical Library), London, 1954

Ars dicendi / Rhetoric, Classical / Figures

*5. 55 BC CICERO, *De Oratore,* tr. E. W. Sutton and H. Rackham (Loeb Classical Library), 2 v., London, 1942

◈

Sel., Dudley Bailey, *Essays on Rhetoric,* New York, 1965, pp. 84–101

Ars dicendi / Rhetoric, Classical / Types

6. 46 BC CICERO, *Brutus,* tr. G. L. Hendrickson (Loeb Classical Library), London, 1939

Rhetoric / Oratory / Orators

7. 46 BC CICERO, *Orator,* tr. H. M. Hubbell (Loeb Classical Library), London, 1939

Ars dicendi / Rhetoric, Classical

8. c.20 BC HORACE, *Ars Poetica,* tr. H. Rushton Fairclough (Loeb Classical Library), London, 1926

Poetry / Ars dicendi / Diction / Innovation / Revision

9. AD 1C DEMETRIUS, *On Style,* tr. W. Rhys Roberts (Loeb Classical Library), London, 1927

Ars dicendi / Types

*10. AD c.95 QUINTILIAN, *Institutio Oratoria,* tr. H. E. Butler (Loeb Classical Library), 4 v., London, 1920

◈

Sel., Dudley Bailey, *Essays on Rhetoric,* New York, 1965, pp. 102–106

Ars dicendi / Rhetoric, Classical

11. AD 1–2C *Longinus on the Sublime,* tr. W. Hamilton Fyfe (Loeb Classical Library), London, 1927

◈

Repr., Lane Cooper, *Theories of Style,* New York, 1907, pp. 97–159

Ars dicendi

12. 1553 WILSON, Thomas, *The Arte of Rhetorique,* ed. Robert Hood Bowers, Gainesville, Fla., 1962

Ars dicendi / Rhetoric, Renaissance / English prose, 16C / Reform, vocabulary

*13. 1570 ASCHAM, Roger, *The Scholemaster,* ed. W. Aldis Wright (*English Works*), Cambridge, 1904

◈

Sel., G. Gregory Smith, *Elizabethan Critical Essays,* Oxford, 1904, Vol. I, pp. 1–45

Ars dicendi / Models / Types

*14. 1589 PUTTENHAM, George, *The Arte of English Poesie,* ed. G. D. Willcock and A. Walker, Cambridge, 1936

◈

Sel., G. Gregory Smith, *Elizabethan Critical Essays,* Oxford, 1904, Vol. II, pp. 1–193

Poetry / Figures / Vocabulary

*15. c.1620 JONSON, Ben, *Timber, or Discoveries,* ed. C. H. Herford, Percy and Evelyn Simpson (*Ben Jonson*), Oxford, 1947, Vol. VIII, pp. 555–649

◈

Sel., J. E. Spingarn, *Critical Essays of the Seventeenth Century,* London, 1908, Vol. I, pp. 17–64

Rhetoric / Mentis character / Diction / Metaphor / Types

16. 1667 SPRAT, Thomas, *The History of the Royal Society of London,* London, 1667

◈

Sel., J. E. Spingarn, *Critical Essays of the Seventeenth Century,* London, 1908, Vol. II, pp. 112–119

English prose, 17C / Reform / Plain style

17. 1698 HUGHES, John, "Of Style," *Poems on Several Occasions, with some Select Essays in Prose,* London, 1735, Vol. I, pp. 247–255

◈

Repr., Willard Higley Durham, *Critical Essays of the Eighteenth Century, 1700–1725,* New York, 1961, pp. 79–85

Ars dicendi / Ideals, 17C / English prose, 17C

18. 1741 HUME, David, "Of Simplicity and Refinement in Writing," *Essays Moral, Political and Literary* (World's Classics), Oxford, 1963, pp. 196–201

English prose, 18C / Ideals / Simplicity

*19. 1753 BUFFON, Georges Louis Leclerc, Comte de, "Discours à l'Académie Française," *Pages Choisies,* Paris, 1934, pp. 65–74

◈

Eng. tr. repr., Lane Cooper, *Theories of Style,* New York, 1907, pp. 169–179

Definition / Ideals

20. 1762–3 SMITH, Adam, *Lectures on Rhetoric and Belles Lettres,* ed. John M. Lothian, London, 1963

Rhetoric / Ideals

*21. 1776 CAMPBELL, George, *The Philosophy of Rhetoric,* ed. L. F. Bitzer, Carbondale, Ill., 1963

◈

Sel., Dudley Bailey, *Essays on Rhetoric,* New York, 1965, pp. 120–133

Ars dicendi / Ideals / Eloquence

22. 1777 PRIESTLEY, Joseph, *A Course of Lectures on Oratory and Criticism,* ed. Vincent M. Bevilacqua and Richard Murphy, Carbondale, Ill., 1965

Rhetoric / Topics / Amplification / Figurative language / Metaphor / Figures / Word order

*23. 1783 BLAIR, Hugh, *Lectures on Rhetoric and Belles Lettres,* ed. Harold F. Harding, 2 v., Carbondale, Ill., 1965

◈

Sel., Dudley Bailey, *Essays on Rhetoric,* New York, 1965, pp. 107–119

Rhetoric / Ars dicendi / Oratory / Addison / Swift

24. 1821–2 HAZLITT, William, "On Familiar Style," *Table Talk,* London, 1821–2, Vol. II, Essay 8

◈

Repr., *Selected Essays of William Hazlitt,* ed. Geoffrey Keynes, New York, 1930, pp. 474–482

English prose, 19C / Familiar style / Slang / Diction / Archaism

25. 1826 HAZLITT, William, "On the Prose Style of Poets," *The Plain Speaker,* London, 1826, Vol. I, pp. 3–30

◈

Repr., *Selected Essays of William Hazlitt,* ed. Geoffrey Keynes, New York, 1930, pp. 482–500

English prose / Verse-prose / Poetical style /Word order

*26. 1828 WHATELY, Richard, *Elements of Rhetoric,* ed. Douglas Ehninger, Carbondale, Ill., 1963

Ars dicendi / Rhetoric / Ideals

27. 1840–1 DE QUINCEY, Thomas, "Style," *Blackwood's Magazine,* XLVIII (1840), 1–17, 387–398, 508–521; XLIX (1841), 214–228

◈

(Continued)

Repr., William T. Brewster, *Representative Essays on the Theory of Style,* New York, 1905, pp. 27–166

Definition / Theory / Rhetoric

28. 1846 POE, Edgar Allan, "The Philosophy of Composition," *Graham's American Monthly Magazine of Literature and Art,* XXVIII (1846), 163–167

Creative process / Composition / Poetry / Rhetoric / Poetics

29. 1851 SCHOPENHAUER, Arthur, "On Style," *The Art of Literature,* tr. T. Bailey Saunders, Ann Arbor, Mich., 1960, pp. 11–30

◈

Repr., Lane Cooper, *Theories of Style,* New York, 1907, pp. 251–269

Ideals / Ars dicendi / Reform

*30. 1852 SPENCER, Herbert, "The Philosophy of Style," *Westminster Review,* LVIII (1852), 435–459

◈

Repr., Dudley Bailey, *Essays on Rhetoric,* New York, 1965, pp. 147–172

Economy principle / Expressiveness / Saxonism / Vocabulary / Concreteness

31. 1858 NEWMAN, John Henry, "Literature," *The Idea of a University,* ed. George N. Shuster, Garden City, N.Y., 1959, pp. 263–283

◈

Repr., William T. Brewster, *Representative Essays on the Theory of Style,* New York, 1905, pp. 1–26

Ideals / Writing-speech / Theory

32. 1865 LEWES, George Henry, "The Principles of Success in Literature," *Fortnightly Review,* II (1865), 257–268, 697–710

◈

Repr., Lane Cooper, *Theories of Style,* New York, 1907, pp. 312–363

Ars dicendi / Ideals / Theory

33. 1866 BAIN, Alexander, *English Composition and Rhetoric,* London, 1866

Ars dicendi / Rhetoric / Figures / Qualities / Models

34. 1874–1902 BUTLER, Samuel, *Samuel Butler's Notebooks,* ed. Geoffrey Keynes and Brian Hill, London, 1951

Ideals / Formation

35. 1875 MACBETH, John Walker Vilant, *The Might and Mirth of Literature,* New York, 1875

Figurative language / Rhetoric / Oratory / Language / Figures

36. 1881 MATHEWS, William, "Literary Style," *Literary Style and Other Essays,* Chicago, 1881, pp. 5–53

Value / Originality / Ornate form / National style / Personality / Qualities

37. 1885 STEVENSON, Robert Louis, "On Some Technical Elements of Style in Literature," *Contemporary Review,* XLVII (1885), 548–561

◈

Repr., Lane Cooper, *Theories of Style,* New York, 1907, pp. 364–385

Ideals / Patterning

38. 1888 PATER, Walter, "Style," *Fortnightly Review,* L (1888), 728–743

Pub., *Appreciations, With an Essay on Style,* New York, 1905, pp. 1–36

◈

(Continued)

Repr., Lane Cooper, *Theories of Style,* New York, 1907, pp. 386–413

Value / Ideals

39. 1890 SYMONDS, John Addington, "Notes on Style," *Essays, Speculative and Suggestive,* 3d. ed., London, 1907, pp. 166–236

Definition / Theory / Ars dicendi / National style / English prose / Personality / Value

40. 1897 RALEIGH, Walter, *Style,* London, 1897

◈

Sel., Paul C. Wermuth, *Modern Essays on Writing and Style,* New York, 1964, pp. 79–84

Ideals / Ars dicendi

41. 1898 HARRISON, Frederic, "On Style in English Prose," *Nineteenth Century,* XLIII (1898), 932–942 Pub., *Tennyson, Ruskin, Mill, and Other Literary Estimates,* London, 1902, pp. 149–165

◈

Repr., Lane Cooper, *Theories of Style,* New York, 1907, pp. 435–452

Value / Natural style / Ars dicendi

41a 1899 GAYLEY, Charles Mills, and Fred Newton SCOTT, "Principles of Literature: Theory of Literature," *An Introduction to the Methods and Materials of Literary Criticism,* Boston, 1899, pp. 200–247

Principles / Survey / Criticism / Aesthetics

42. 1900 BRUNETIERE, Ferdinand, "Style," *La Grande Encyclopédie,* Vol. xxx, Paris, 1886ff.

Theory / Ideals

43. 1902 ALBALAT, Antoine, *La formation du style,* Paris, 1902

Ars dicendi / Formation / Models / Rhetoric

44. 1902 GOURMONT, Remy de, *Le problème du style,* Paris, 1902

Organic theory / Definition / Models / Personality

45. 1904 HENDRICKSON, G. L., "The Peripatetic Mean of Style and the Three Stylistic Characters," *American Journal of Philology,* XXV (1904), 125–146

Aristotle / Middle style / Rhetoric, Classical / Levels / Characters, stylistic

46. 1905 HENDRICKSON, G. L., "The Origin and Meaning of the Ancient Characters of Style," *American Journal of Philology,* XXVI (1905), 249–290

Characters, stylistic / Grand style / Middle style / Plain style / Rhetoric, Classical / Aristole / Cicero

47. 1905 MERCHANT, Frank Ivan, "Seneca the Philosopher and His Theory of Style," *American Journal of Philology,* XXVI (1905), 44–59

Theory / Rhetoric, Classical / Seneca

*48. 1909 CROCE, Benedetto, *Aesthetic,* tr. D. Ainslie, New York, 1958

Theory / Rhetoric / Organic theory / Aesthetics

49. 1910 GOSSE, Edmund, "Style," *Encyclopedia Britannica,* Vol. XXV, 11 ed., Cambridge, 1910–11

Definition / Theory / Ars dicendi

50. 1913 BREWSTER, William Tenney, *Writing English Prose,* New York, 1913

Ars dicendi / Composition / Ideals

*51. 1921 SAPIR, Edward, "Language and Literature," *Language*, New York, 1921, pp. 236–247

◈

Repr., Paul C. Wermuth, *Modern Essays on Writing and Style*, New York, 1964, pp. 32–38

Norm, linguistic / Definition

52. 1921 SARTON, George, "Science and Style," *Scribner's Magazine*, LXIX (1921), 755–759

Definition / Ideal form / Aesthetics

*53. 1922 MURRY, J. Middleton, *The Problem of Style*, London, 1956

◈

Sel., Paul C. Wermuth, *Modern Essays on Writing and Style*, New York, 1964, pp. 206–216

Theory / Definition

54. 1924 BALDWIN, Charles Sears, *Ancient Rhetoric and Poetic*, Gloucester, Mass., 1959

Rhetoric, Classical / Figures / Theory

55. 1924 BROWNELL, W. C., *The Genius of Style*, New York, 1924

Definition / English prose / Ideals / Personality

56. 1925 HULME, T. E., *Notes on Language and Style*, ed. Herbert Read, Seattle, Wash., 1929

Analogy / Imagery / Expressive theory / Organic theory

57. 1925 VOSSLER, Karl, *The Spirit of Language in Civilization*, tr. Oscar Oeser, London, 1951

Sociology / National style / Linguistics

58. 1927 SAPIR, Edward, "Speech as a Personality Trait," *Selected Writings of Edward Sapir*, ed. David

G. Mandelbaum, Berkeley and Los Angeles, 1958, pp. 533–543

Theory / Speech / Personality / Norm, linguistic

59. 1928 BALDWIN, Charles Sears, *Medieval Rhetoric and Poetic,* Gloucester, Mass., 1959

◈

Sel., Joseph Schwartz and John A. Rycenga, *The Province of Rhetoric,* New York, 1965, pp. 158–172

Rhetoric, Classical / Figures / Composition

60. 1928 BARFIELD, Owen, *Poetic Diction: A Study in Meaning,* 2d ed., New York, 1964

Diction / Poetry / Imagery / Meaning

61. 1928 PALMER, H. E., "Word-Values," *Psyche,* IX (1928), 12–25

Vocabulary / Expressive theory / Connotation / Lexical style

*62. 1928 READ, Herbert, *English Prose Style,* Boston, 1955

◈

Sel., Paul C. Wermuth, *Modern Essays on Writing and Style,* New York, 1964, pp. 39–55, 115–123

Ars dicendi / Theory / Types

63. 1930 MONTAGUE, C. E., "Only Too Clear," *A Writer's Notes on His Trade,* London, 1930, pp. 71–92

◈

Repr., Paul C. Wermuth, *Modern Essays on Writing and Style,* New York, 1964, pp. 241–252

Clarity / Obscurity / Unconsciousness

64\. 1931 D'ALTON, J. F., "Aspects of the Theory of Style," *Roman Literary Theory and Criticism,* New York, 1962, pp. 68–140

Rhetoric, Roman / Levels / Figures / Decorum

65\. 1934 ALLPORT, F. H., L. WALKER, and E. LATHERS, "Written Composition and Characteristics of Personality," *Archives of Psychology,* No. 173, New York, 1934

Definition / Composition / Personality

66\. 1934 ATKINS, J. W. H., *Literary Criticism in Antiquity,* 2 v., London, 1952

Rhetoric, Classical / Theory / Definition / Figures

66a 1935 BURKE, Kenneth, "Style," *Permanence and Change,* 2d rev. ed., Indianapolis, 1965, pp. 50–58

Value / Sociology / Reflection theory / Technology

*66b 1935 ZIPF, George Kingsley, *The Psycho-Biology of Language: An Introduction to Dynamic Philology,* Cambridge, Mass., 1965

Language / Psychology / Statistics / Phonemes / Words / Accent / Sentence / Behavior / Quantitative methods

67\. 1936 ALLPORT, Gordon W. and Henry S. ODBERT, "Trait-Names: A Psycho-lexical Study," *Psychological Monographs,* XLVII (1936), 1–171

Personality / Trait-names / Psychology, nomenclature

*68. 1936 RICHARDS, I. A., *The Philosophy of Rhetoric,* New York, 1965

Rhetoric / Metaphor / Semantics / Theory

69\. 1939 BALDWIN, Charles Sears, *Renaissance Literary Theory and Practice,* Gloucester, Mass., 1959

Rhetoric, Classical / Rhetoric, Renaissance / Theory

70. 1939 LEWIS, C. S., and E. M. W. TILLYARD, *The Personal Heresy: A Controversy,* London, 1965

Personality / Fallacy, biographical / Persona

71. 1939 MANN, Elizabeth L., "The Problem of Originality in English Literary Criticism 1750–1800," *Philological Quarterly,* XVIII (1939), 97–118

Ideals, 18C / Originality / Theory / English prose, 18C

72. 1941 SAMUEL, Viscount, *On Style,* London, 1941

Ars dicendi / Ideals

73. 1942 ALONSO, Amado, "The Stylistic Interpretation of Literary Texts," *Modern Language Notes,* LVII (1942), 489–496

Organic theory / Diction / Expressive theory

74. 1942 MCKEON, Richard, "Rhetoric in the Middle Ages," *Speculum,* XVII (1942), 1–32

◈

Repr., Joseph Schwartz and John A. Rycenga, *The Province of Rhetoric,* New York, 1965, pp. 172–212

Rhetoric, medieval / Rhetoric, decline / Rhetoric, history / Logic / Cicero

75. 1943 ATKINS, J. W. H., *English Literary Criticism: The Medieval Phase,* London, 1943

Rhetoric, Classical / Ideals / Composition

76. 1947 ATKINS, J. W. H., *English Literary Criticism: The Renascence,* London, 1947

Rhetoric, Classical / Theory / Ideals / Poetics

*77. 1948 CURTIUS, Ernst Robert, *European Literature and the Latin Middle Ages,* tr. Willard R. Trask, New York, 1963

Rhetoric, medieval / Figures / Topics / Metaphor

78. 1948 DEVOTO, Giacomo, "Introduction à la stylistique," *Mélanges de philologie, de littérature et d'histoire anciennes offerts à J. Marouzeau . . .*, Paris, 1948, pp. 125–139

Stylistic function / Affectivity / Deviation, linguistic / Grammar / Choice

79. 1948 OPPENHEIMER, J. R., "A Definition of Style," *The Limits of Language,* ed. Walker Gibson, New York, 1962, pp. 50–51

Definition / Value / Impressionism

80. 1948 STUTTERHEIM, C. F. P., "Modern Stylistics, I," *Lingua,* I (1948), 410–426

Theory / Typology / Survey

81. 1949 FLESCH, Rudolf, *The Art of Readable Writing,* New York, 1962

Ars dicendi / Ideals

82. 1949 LASSWELL, Harold D., "Style in the Language of Politics," *Language of Politics: Studies in Quantitative Semantics,* New York, 1949, pp. 20–39

Political language / Audience expectation / Effectiveness / Terseness / Prolixity / Repetition / Reflection theory

*83. 1949 WELLEK, René and Austin WARREN, "Style and Stylistics," *Theory of Literature,* New York, 1949, pp. 177–189

Theory / Definition / Methods

83a 1950 WIMSATT, W. K., Jr., "Verbal Style: Logical and Counterlogical," *PMLA,* LXV (1950), 5–20

◈

Repr., *The Verbal Icon,* New York, 1960, pp. 201–217
(*See* No. 100)
Definition / Form-content / Levels / Semantics

84. 1951 ATKINS, J. W. H., *English Literary Criticism: 17th and 18th Centuries,* London, 1954
Theory / Ideals / English prose, 17C–18C

85. 1951 BRUNEAU, Charles, "La stylistique," *Romance Philology,* V (1951), pp. 1–14
Theory / Definition / Methods / Survey

86. 1951 DRESDEN, S., "La notion de style en littérature et dans les beaux-arts," *Actes du cinquième congrès international des langues et littératures modernes, mars 1951,* Florence, 1955, pp. 11–19
Theory / Aesthetics

87. 1951 FIRTH, J. R., "Modes of Meaning," *Essays and Studies,* N. S. IV (1951), 118–149
◈
Repr., *Papers in Linguistics: 1934–1951,* London, 1957, pp. 190–215
Semantics / Context / English prose

88. 1951 HARKINS, William E., "Slavic Formalist Theories in Literary Scholarship," *Word,* VII (1951), 175–185
Theory / Form-content / Formalism, Slavic

88a 1951 WIMSATT, W. K., Jr., "The Substantive Level," *Sewanee Review,* LIX (1951), 1–23
◈
Repr., *The Verbal Icon,* New York, 1960, pp. 133–151
(*See* No. 100)

Definition / Form-content / Levels / Semantic norm / Deviation

89. 1952 CRADDOCK, Sister Clare Eileen, *Style Theories as Found in Stylistic Studies of Romance Scholars (1900–1950)*, Washington, D.C., 1952

Theory / Definition / Survey / Vossler / Bally / Spitzer

90. 1952 FLYDAL, Leiv, "Remarques sur certains rapports entre le style et l'état de langue," *Norsk Tidsskrift for Sprogvidenskap*, XVI (1952), 241–258

State, linguistic / Diachronism / Archaism / Levels

91. 1952 STUTTERHEIM, C. F. P., "Modern Stylistics, II," *Lingua*, III (1952), 52–68

Elements / Problems / Poetry / Psychology / Rhythm

92. 1953 ABRAMS, M. H., "Literature as a Revelation of Personality," *The Mirror and the Lamp*, New York, 1958, pp. 226–235

Theory / Definition / Aesthetics / Personality / Reflection theory

93. 1953 ENTWISTLE, W. J., *Aspects of Language*, London, 1953

Norm, linguistic / Affectivity / Theory

94. 1953 ERLICH, Victor, "The Russian Formalist Movement," *Partisan Review*, XX (1953), 282–296

Formalism, Slavic / Linguistics / Theory / Jakobson

95. 1953 JANSON, H. W., *Style and Styles*, New York, 1953

Theory / Definition / Aesthetics / Typology / National style / Stylization

96. 1953 SAYCE, R. A., *Style in French Prose,* Oxford, 1958

Definition / Methods / French language

97. 1953 SCHAPIRO, Meyer, "Style," *Anthropology Today,* ed. A. L. Kroeber, Chicago, 1953, pp. 287–312

Aesthetics / Anthropology / Typology / Sources

98. 1953 SPITZER, Leo, "Language—The Basis of Science, Philosophy and Poetry," *Studies in Intellectual History,* ed. George Boas, *et al.,* Baltimore, 1953, pp. 67–93

◈

Repr., *Bobbs-Merrill Reprint Series in Language and Linguistics,* No. 85

Linguistic philosophy / Linguistics / Metalinguistics / Philology

*99. 1953 WEAVER, Richard M., *The Ethics of Rhetoric,* New York, 1964

◈

Sel., Joseph Schwartz and John A. Rycenga, *The Province of Rhetoric,* New York, 1965, pp. 275–292, 311–329

Rhetoric, modern / Plato / Burke / Lincoln / Milton / Sentences / Grammar / Parts of speech / Argument / Oratory / Semantics

100. 1954 WIMSATT, W. K., Jr., *The Verbal Icon,* New York, 1960

Meaning / Imagery / Intention / Affectivity / Form-content / Metrics / Poetry / Pope / Rhetoric

*101. 1955 LUCAS, F. L., *Style,* London, 1955

◈

Sel., Paul C. Wermuth, *Modern Essays on Writing and Style,* New York, 1964, pp. 3–16, 124–140

Ars dicendi / Ideals / English prose

102. 1955 WELLEK, René, *A History of Modern Criticism: 1750–1950,* 4 v., New Haven, 1955, 1965
Theory / Ideals

102a 1956 HILL, Archibald A., "Poetry and Stylistics," *Essays in Literary Analysis,* Austin, 1965, pp. 50–62
Predictability / Analogy / Levels / Meaning / Interpretation / Linguistics

103. 1956 HOWELL, Wilbur Samuel, *Logic and Rhetoric in England, 1500–1700,* New York, 1961
Rhetoric, Renaissance / Wilson, Thomas / Ramus / Logic

104. 1956 MUNRO, Thomas, "Style in the Arts: A Method of Stylistic Analysis," *Toward Science in Aesthetics,* New York, 1956, pp. 192–226
Aesthetics / Definition / Classification

105. 1956 SPRINGER, George P., "Language and Music: Parallels and Divergencies," *For Roman Jakobson,* ed. Morris Halle, *et al.,* The Hague, 1956, pp. 504–513
Music / Code / Language

106. 1957 CHERRY, Colin, *On Human Communication,* Cambridge, Mass. and New York, 1957
Communication / Information theory / Linguistics / Quantitative method

*107. 1957 KROEBER, A. L., *Style and Civilizations,* Berkeley and Los Angeles, 1963
Theory / Anthropology

107a 1957 SHAHN, Ben, "The Shape of Content," *The Shape of Content,* New York, 1957, pp. 62–83
Form-content / Aesthetics / Criticism

*108. 1958 BEARDSLEY, Monroe C., "Style: Semantic and Phonetic," *Aesthetics,* New York, 1958, pp. 220–237, 254–260

Meaning / Value / Sounds / Poetry

108a 1958 DEVOTO, Giacomo, "Stilistica e critica," *La critica stilistica e il barocco letterario,* Florence, 1958

Theory / Ideals / Aesthetics / Grammar / Linguistics / Impressionism

109. 1958 HATZFELD, Helmut, "Recent Italian Stylistic Theory and Stylistic Criticism," *Studia Philologica et Litteraria in Honorem L. Spitzer,* ed. A. G. Hatcher et K. L. Selig, Berne, 1958, pp. 227–243

Stylistics, Italian / Theory / Aesthetics / Method / Survey

109a 1958 HILL, Archibald A., "Beyond the Sentence," *Introduction to Linguistic Structures,* New York, 1958, pp. 406–417

Linguistics / Macrostylistics / Semantics / Redundancy / Situation

110. 1959 FERGUSON, Charles W., *Say It With Words,* New York, 1959

Ars dicendi / Ideals / Formation

111. 1959 FOGARTY, Daniel, *Roots for a New Rhetoric,* New York, 1959

◈ Sel., Joseph Schwartz and John A. Rycenga, *The Province of Rhetoric,* New York, 1965, pp. 345–366

Theory / Rhetoric / General semantics / Burke, K. / Richards, I. A.

112. 1959 MAROUZEAU, J., "Nature, degrés et qualités de l'expression stylistique," *Stil- und Formprob-*

(*Continued*)

leme in der Literatur, ed. Paul Böckmann, Heidelberg, 1959, pp. 15–18

Theory / Definition / Stylistic function

*113. 1959 OHMANN, Richard M., "Prolegomena to the Analysis of Prose Style," *Style in Prose Fiction,* ed. Harold C. Martin, New York, 1959, pp. 1–24

◈ Repr., *Bobbs-Merrill Reprint Series in Language and Linguistics,* No. 70

Theory / Epistemology / Aesthetics / Croce / Form-content

*114. 1959 RIFFATERRE, Michael, "Criteria for Style Analysis," *Word,* XV (1959), pp. 154–174

Definition / Affectivity / Information theory / Norm, linguistic

114a 1959 WARBURG, Jeremy, "Some Aspects of Style," *The Teaching of English,* ed. Randolph Quirk and A. H. Smith, London, 1964, pp. 36–59

Vocabulary / Synonymity / Definition / Teaching / Ars dicendi

115. 1959 WIMSATT, William K., Jr., and Cleanth BROOKS, *Literary Criticism: A Short History,* New York, 1959

Rhetoric, history / Dryden / Johnson / Wordsworth / Croce / Theory

115a 1960 DELBOUILLE, Paul, "A propos de la définition du fait de style," *Cahiers d'analyse textuelle,* II (1960), 94–104

Definition / Norm / Deviation / Quantitative methods

116\. 1960 QUENNELL, Peter, "Stylists," *The Sign of the Fish,* New York, 1960, pp. 80–96

Value / Moore, George / Plain-ornate

117\. 1960 QUINE, Willard Van Orman, *Word and Object,* Cambridge, Mass., 1964

Semantics / Epistemology / Linguistic philosophy

*118. 1960 RIFFATERRE, Michael, "Stylistic Context," *Word,* XVI (1960), 207–218

Definition / Context / Information theory / Deviation, linguistic

118a 1961 DELBOUILLE, Paul, "Retour à la notion d'écart," *Cahiers d'analyse textuelle,* III (1961), 105–108

(*See* No. 115a)

119\. 1961 GORNY, Wojciech, "Text Structure Against the Background of Language Structure," *Poetics,* Warsaw, 1961, pp. 25–37

Linguistic stylistics / Methods / Text style

120\. 1961 MASSON, David I., "Sound-Repetition Terms," *Poetics,* Warsaw, 1961, pp. 189–199

Sounds / Repetition / Poetics / Rhetorical terms / Terminology

121\. 1961 MCINTOSH, Angus, "Patterns and Ranges," *Language,* XXXVII (1961), 325–337

◈

Repr., Angus McIntosh and M. A. K. Halliday, *Patterns of Language,* London, 1966, pp. 183–199

Grammaticality / Collocation / Lexical compatibility / Meaning / Reference / Context

122. 1961 SKWARCZYNSKA, Stefania, "La stylisation et sa place dans la science de la littérature," *Poetics,* Warsaw, 1961, pp. 53–70

Stylization / Consciousness / Stylistic devices / Formalism / Theory

123. 1961 STANKIEWICZ, Edward, "Poetic and Non-Poetic Language in Their Interrelation," *Poetics,* Warsaw, 1961, pp. 11–23

Poetical style / Poetics / Linguistics / Grammatical tropes

124. 1961 STUTTERHEIM, Cornelis F. P., "Poetry and Prose, Their Interrelations and Transitional Forms," *Poetics,* Warsaw, pp. 225–237

Poetry / Definition / Poetics / Prose-verse / Prosody

125. 1962 CHATMAN, Seymour, "Linguistic Style, Literary Style and Performance: Some Distinctions," *Report of the Eleventh Annual Round Table Meeting on Linguistics and Language Studies,* ed. Bernard Choseed, Washington, D.C., 1962, pp. 73–81

Speech / Phonemics / Meaning / Idiosyncratic style

126. 1962 GIBSON, Walker, "A Note on Style and the Limits of Language," *The Limits of Language,* ed. Walker Gibson, New York, 1962

Definition / Personality / Consciousness / Vocabulary

127. 1962 GLEASON, H. A., Jr., "What Is English?" *College Composition and Communication,* XIII (1962), 1–10

Definition / Composition / Norm, linguistic

*128. 1962 SAYCE, R. A., "The Definition of the Term 'Style'," *Proceedings of the Third Congress of the*

International Comparative Literature Association, The Hague, 1962, pp. 156–166

Definition / Methods / Terminology

129. 1962 ULLMANN, Stephen, *Semantics,* Oxford, 1962

Semantics / Vocabulary / Meaning / Affectivity

130. 1962 ZUMTHOR, Paul, "Stylistique et poétique," Pierre Guiraud, *et al., Style et littérature,* The Hague, 1962, pp. 27–38

Poetics / Poetical style / Information theory / Ambiguity

130a 1963 DEVOTO, Giacomo, *Linguistics and Literary Criticism,* tr. M. F. Edgerton, New York, 1963

Stylistics, Italian / Definition / Criticism / Grammar / Tradition

131. 1963 FRYE, Northrop, *The Well-Tempered Critic,* Bloomington, Ind., 1963

Rhetoric / Genre / Types / Levels

132. 1963 HALL, Robert A., Jr., *Idealism in Romance Linguistics,* Ithaca, N.Y., 1963

Idealism / Theory / Croce / Spitzer / Vossler / Linguistic stylistics

133. 1963 KOCH, Walter Alfred, "On the Principles of Stylistics," *Lingua,* XII (1963), 411–422

Linguistic stylistics / Semantics / Contrast / Context / Substitution / Matrix / Differentials

134. 1963 LAUSBERG, Heinrich, *Elemente der Literarischen Rhetorik,* Munich, 1963

Rhetorical, Classical / Figures

135. 1963 LEEMAN, A. D., *Orationis Ratio: The Stylistic Theories and Practice of the Roman Orators Historians and Philosophers,* 2 v., Amsterdam, 1963

Rhetorical, Classical / Rhetoric, history / Theory / Oratory

136. 1963 WELLEK, René, *Concepts of Criticism,* New Haven, 1963

Theory / Croce

137. 1964 ENKVIST, Nils Erik, "On Defining Style: An Essay in Applied Linguistics," *Linguistics and Style,* ed. John Spencer, London, 1964, pp. 3–56

Definition / Linguistics / Theory / Methods

138. 1964 GEORGE, F. H., *Semantics,* London, 1964

Semantics / Linguistic philosophy / Information theory

138a 1964 GRAY, Barbara Bennison, "An Inquiry into the Problem of Style: A Negative Experiment," *Dissertation Abstracts,* XXV (1965), 5257–5258

Definition / Theory / Method / Stylistic function / Langue-parole

139. 1964 LEVIN, Samuel R., "Poetry and Grammaticalness," *Proceedings of the Ninth International Congress of Linguists,* ed. Horace G. Lunt, The Hague, 1964, pp. 308–315

Generative grammar / Poetry / Grammaticality / Originality

140. 1964 RIFFATERRE, Michael, "The Stylistic Function," *Proceedings of the Ninth International Congress of Linguists,* ed. Horace G. Lunt, The Hague, 1964, pp. 316–323

Affectivity / Information theory / Stylistic function

140a 1964 SONTAG, Susan, "Against Interpretation," *Evergreen Review,* VIII (1964), 76–80, 93
◈
Repr., *Against Interpretation,* New York, 1966, pp. 3–14

Imitation / Interpretation / Form-content

*141. 1964 ULLMANN, Stephen, *Language and Style,* Oxford, 1964

Semantics / Meaning / Affectivity / Theory / Definition / Methods / Imagery / Vocabulary

142. 1964 WINTER, Werner, "Styles as Dialects," *Proceedings of the Ninth International Congress of Linguists,* ed. Horace G. Lunt, The Hague, 1964, pp. 324–330

Dialect / Definition / Quantitative methods / Statistics

*142a 1965 GLEASON, H. A., Jr., "Literary Form and Style," *Linguistics and English Grammars,* New York, 1965, pp. 419–439

Linguistics / Poetics / Prosody / Phonology / Choice / Grammar / Diction / Patterning / Foregrounding

143. 1965 GRUBE, G. M. A., *The Greek and Roman Critics,* Toronto, 1965

Rhetoric, Classical / Language / Theory / Rhetoric, history

144. 1965 HADAS, Moses, "Style the Repository," *American Scholar,* XXXIV (1965), 213–219

Value / Grand style / Traditional style

144a 1965 LEVIN, Samuel R., 'Internal and External Deviation in Poetry," *Word,* XXI (1965), 225–237

Deviation / Generative grammar / Grammaticalness

145. 1965 MCINTOSH, Angus, "Saying," *Review of English Literature,* VI (1965), 9–20

Context / Situation / Linguistics

146. 1965 MILIC, Louis T., "Theories of Style and Their Implications for the Teaching of Composition," *College Composition and Communication,* XVI (1965), 66–69, 126

Theory / Composition / Teaching / Form-content

147. 1965 MOWATT, D. G., and P. F. DEMBOWSKI, "Literary Study and Linguistics," *Canadian Journal of Linguistics,* XI (1965), 40–62

Linguistics / Dualism / Method / Form-content / Metrics

148. 1965 SONTAG, Susan, "On Style," *Partisan Review,* XXXII (1965), 543–560

Definition / Form-content / Ornate form / Typology / Convention

149. 1965 THORNE, James Peter, "Stylistics and Generative Grammars," *Journal of Linguistics,* I (1965), 49–59

Deviation, linguistic / Norm, linguistic / Generative grammar / Poetry / Grammaticalness

150. 1965 ULLMANN Stephen, "Style and Personality," *Review of English Literature,* VI (1965), 21–31

Personality / Survey

151. 1965 WARBURG, Jeremy, "Idiosyncratic Style," *Review of English Literature,* VI (1965), 56–65

Idiosyncrasy / Milton / Hopkins / Lyly / Faulkner / James, Henry

152. 1966 BAKER, Sheridan, *The Complete Stylist,* New York, 1966

Ars dicendi / Purism / Errors / Figures

152a 1966 BEARDSLEY, Monroe C., "Style and Good Style," *Reflections on High School English,* ed. Gary Tate, Tulsa, Okla., 1966, pp. 91–105

Value / Synonymity / Form-content / Teaching

153. 1966 BROWN, Huntington, *Prose Styles: Five Primary Types,* Minneapolis, 1966

English prose / Levels / Typology / Rhetoric, Classical

154. 1966 FOWLER, Roger, "Linguistic Theory and the Study of Literature," *Essays on Style and Language,* ed. Roger Fowler, London, 1966, pp. 1–29

Linguistic stylistics / Interpretation / Comparison

154a 1966 GRAY, Bennison, "The Lesson of Leo Spitzer," *Modern Language Review,* LXI (1966), 547–555

Definition / Form-content / Reflection theory / Spitzer

155. 1966 HUGHES, Richard E., and P. Albert DUHAMEL, *Principles of Rhetoric,* Englewood Cliffs, N.J., 1966

Ars dicendi / Rhetoric / Analysis

156. 1966 LEECH, G. N., "Linguistics and the Figures of Rhetoric," *Essays on Language and Style,* ed. Roger Fowler, London, 1966, pp. 135–156

Rhetoric / Figures / Linguistic analysis / Metaphor / Deviation, linguistic / Foregrounding / Interpretation

157. 1966 MCINTOSH, Angus, "Some Thoughts on Style," *Patterns of Language,* London, 1966, pp. 83–97

Situational context / Appropriateness / Adequacy / Deviation, linguistic / Convention / Norm, linguistic

158. 1967 MILIC, Louis T., "Against the Typology of Styles," *Essays in the Language of Literature,* ed. Seymour Chatman and S. R. Levin, Boston, 1967, pp. 442–450

Typology / Period style / English prose, Restoration

158a 1967 ROBERTSON, Duncan, "The Dichotomy of Form and Content," *College English,* XXVIII (1967), 273–279

Aesthetics / Form-content / Structure / Paraphrase

158b 1967 STOEHR, Taylor, "Writing as Thinking," *College English,* XXVIII (1967), 411–421

Form-content / Conceptualization / Composition / Teaching

Part Two

METHODOLOGICAL

159. 1887 MENDENHALL, T. C., "The Characteristic Curves of Composition," *Science,* IX (1887), 237–249

Attribution / Quantitative methods / Graphs / Word-length

160. 1892 SHERMAN, Lucius A., "On Certain Facts and Principles in the Development of Form in Literature," *University of Nebraska Studies,* I (1892), 337–366

Quantitative methods / Sentence-length / English prose / Macaulay

*161. 1893 SHERMAN, Lucius A., *Analytics of Literature,* Boston, 1893

Quantitative methods / Syntax / Vocabulary / Imagery

162. 1901 MENDENHALL, T. C., "A Mechanical Solution of a Literary Problem," *Popular Science Monthly,* LX (1901), 97–105

Attribution / Quantitative methods / Word-length / Shakespeare question

*163. 1903 MORITZ, Robert E., "On the Variation and Functional Relation of Certain Sentence-Constants in Standard Literature," *University of Nebraska Studies,* III (1903), 229–253

Quantitative methods / Statistics / Sherman, L. A. / Sentences

164. 1908 ALBALAT, Antoine, *Le travail du style,* Paris, 1953

Formation / Revision / Correctness

165. 1912 BREWSTER, William Tenney, "Style," *English Composition and Style,* New York, 1912, pp. 175–299

Diction / Sentences / Syntax

166. 1915 MORRIS, Edward P., "A Science of Style," *Transactions and Proceedings of the American Philological Association,* XLVI (1915), 103–118

Objective methods / Psychology / Syntax / Latin

167. 1919 PROUST, Marcel, "L'affaire Lemoine," *Pastiches et mélanges,* Paris, 1935, pp. 11–87

Models / Parody / French literature, 19C

168. 1921 REBOUX, Paul, and Charles MULLER, *A la manière de . . . ,* 2 v., Paris, 1959

Models / Parody

169. 1925 BALLY, Charles, *Le langage et la vie,* 3d ed., Paris, 1962

Linguistics / Contrastive study / Affectivity

*170. 1927 RICKERT, Edith, *New Methods for the Study of Literature,* Chicago, 1927

Quantitative methods / Graphs / Imagery / Vocabulary / Rhythm

171. 1928 CHASSE, Charles, *Styles et physiologie,* Paris, 1928

Physiology / Psychology / Typology / French prose, 19C

*172. 1938 YULE, G. Udny, "On Sentence-Length as a Statistical Characteristic of Style in Prose; with Application to Two Cases of Disputed Authorship," *Biometrika,* XXX (1938), 363–390

Quantitative methods / Statistics / Sentence-length / Attribution

*173. 1940 BODER, David P., "The Adjective-Verb Quotient: A Contribution to the Psychology of Language," *Psychological Record,* III (1940), 309–343

Psychology / Parts of speech / Adjective-verb quotient / Emotion / Personality

*174. 1940 WILLIAMS, C. B., "A Note on the Statistical Analysis of Sentence-Length as a Criterion of Literary Style," *Biometrika,* XXXI (1940), 356–361

Quantitative methods / Statistics / Sentence-length / Attribution

175. 1942 HORNSTEIN, Lillian Herlands, "Analysis of Imagery: A Critique of Literary Method," *PMLA,* LVII (1942), 638–653

Imagery / Quantitative methods / Spurgeon

*176. 1942 SANFORD, Fillmore H., "Speech and Personality," *Psychological Bulletin,* XXXIX (1942), 811–845

Personality / Psychology / Objective methods / Grammar / Disturbed speech

177. 1943 DAVIS, Herbert, "The Canon of Swift," *English Institute Essays, 1942,* New York, 1943, pp. 119–136

Attribution / Canon / Internal evidence / Swift

178. 1944 JOHNSON, Wendell, "Studies in Language Behavior," *Psychological Monographs,* LVI (1944), 1–15

Psychology / Type-token ratio / Quantitative methods / Word-frequency / Disturbed speech

*179. 1944 YULE, G. Udny, *The Statistical Study of Literary Vocabulary,* Cambridge, 1944

Quantitative methods / Statistics / Attribution / Vocabulary / Word-class frequency

*180. 1947 QUENEAU, Raymond, *Exercices de style,* Paris, 1961

◈

Sel., *Language, Style, Ideas,* ed. Sumner Ives and Stephen O. Mitchell, New York, 1964, pp. 223–224

Variations / Form-content / Types / Models

*181. 1948 SPITZER, Leo, *Linguistics and Literary History,* New York, 1962

(*See also* Nos. 154a, 672)

Philology / Psychoanalysis / Philological circle / Diderot / Cervantes / Deviation, linguistic

182\. 1949 HATZFELD, Helmut, "Stylistic Criticism as Art-minded Philology," *Yale French Studies,* II (1949), 62–70

Spitzer / Vossler / Aesthetics / Quantitative methods

*183. 1950 HYTIER, J., "La méthode de M. L. Spitzer," *Romanic Review,* XLI (1950), 42–59 (Rev. of No. 181)

Spitzer / A priori methods / Organic theory / Linguistics

184\. 1950 WIENER, Norbert, *The Human Use of Human Beings: Cybernetics and Society,* New York, 1954

Cybernetics / Information theory / Computers / Nervous system / Brain

*185. 1951 MILLER, George A., *Language and Communication,* New York, 1951

Psychology / Personality / Quantitative methods / Information theory

186\. 1951 ROSTAND, François, *Grammaire et affectivité,* Paris, 1951

Grammar / Affectivity / Psychology / Disturbed speech

187\. 1952 ESTRICH, Robert M., and Hans SPERBER, "Personal Style"; "Personal Style and Period Style: A Victorian Poet," *Three Keys to Language,* New York, 1952, pp. 212–275

Personality / Psychology / Typology / Methods / Tennyson

188\. 1952 FUCKS, William, "On Mathematical Analysis of Style," *Biometrika,* XXXIX (1952), 122–129

Quantitative methods / Statistics / Syllable-counts / Attribution / Entropy function

189. 1952 SPITZER, Leo, "Les théories de la stylistique," *Le français moderne,* XX (1952), 165–168

Philological circle / Objective methods / Scientism

190. 1953 ULLMANN, Stephen, "Psychologie et stylistique," *Journal de psychologie,* XLVI (1953), 133–156

Survey / Bally / Spitzer / Psychology

*191. 1954 GUIRAUD, Pierre, *Les caractères statistiques du vocabulaire,* Paris, 1954

Lexicon / Quantitative methods / Statistics / Parts of speech / Keywords / Baudelaire / Rimbaud / Mallarmé / Apollinaire / Valéry / Claudel / French poetry

192. 1955 BAR-HILLEL, Yehoshua, "Idioms," *Machine Translation of Languages,* ed. William N. Locke and A. D. Booth, Cambridge, Mass. and New York, 1957, pp. 183–193

Idioms / Machine translation / Dictionary / Words

193. 1955 BARRERE, Jean-Bertrand, "Etudes littéraires et caractérologie," *Literature and Science* (Proceedings of the Sixth Triennial Congress, International Federation for Modern Languages and Literatures, 1954), Oxford, 1955, pp. 80–85

Personality / Character types / Syntax

194. 1955 BOOTH, A. Donald, and William N. LOCKE, "Historical Introduction," *Machine Translation of Languages,* ed. William N. Locke and A. D.

Booth, Cambridge, Mass. and New York, 1957, pp. 1–14
Machine translation / Technology / Computers

195. 1955 BULL, William E., Charles AFRICA and Daniel TEICHROEW, "Some Problems of the 'Word'," *Machine Translation of Languages,* ed. William N. Locke and A. D. Booth, Cambridge, Mass. and New York, 1957, pp. 86–103
Words / Computer storage / Machine translation

*196. 1955 DODD, Stuart C., "Model English," *Machine Translation of Languages,* ed. William N. Locke and A. D. Booth, Cambridge, Mass. and New York, 1957, pp. 165–173
English language, revision / Grammar / Artificial language / Information theory / Redundancy

197. 1955 DUFRENOY, Marie-Louise, "The Use of Statistics in Plotting out Literary Trends," *Literature and Science* (Proceedings of the Sixth Triennial Congress, International Federation for Modern Languages and Literatures, 1954), Oxford, 1955, pp. 91–95
Trends, literary / Quantitative methods / Statistics

198. 1955 ESCARPIT, Robert, "Essai d'application d'une méthode de statistique démographique à l'étude de l'histoire littéraire," *Literature and Science* (Proceedings of the Sixth Triennial Congress, International Federation for Modern Languages and Literatures, 1954), Oxford, 1955, pp. 95–98
Quantitative methods / Statistics

199. 1955 GUBERINA, P., "Procédés stylistiques et stylographiques: analyse scientifique et littéraire,"

(Continued)

Literature and Science (Proceedings of the Sixth Triennial Congress, International Federation for Modern Languages and Literatures, 1954), Oxford, 1955, pp. 51–56

Stylographic analysis / Expressive mechanisms / Linguistics

200. 1955 HATZFELD, Helmut, "Methods of Stylistic Investigation," *Literature and Science* (Proceedings of the Sixth Triennial Congress, International Federation for Modern Languages and Literatures, 1954), Oxford, 1955, pp. 44–51

Methods / Survey / Stylistics, historical / Bally / Spitzer / Croce

201. 1955 MARTINI, Fritz, "Persönlichkeitsstil und Zeitstil," *Studium Generale,* VIII (1955), 31–40

Personality / Period style / Typology

202. 1955 RICHENS, R. H., and A. D. BOOTH, "Some Methods of Mechanized Translation," *Machine Translation of Languages,* ed. William N. Locke and A. D. Booth, Cambridge, Mass. and New York, 1957, pp. 24–46

Machine translation / Words / Dictionary / Stems / Grammar / Computers

203. 1955 VINCENT, E. R., "Mechanical Aids for the Study of Language and Literary Style," *Literature and Science* (Proceedings of the Sixth Triennial Congress, International Federation for Modern Languages and Literatures, 1954), Oxford, 1955, pp. 56–60

Objective methods / Quantitative methods / Computers / Poetics / Parts of speech

*204. 1955 WEAVER, Warren, "'Translation," *Machine Translation of Languages,* ed. William N. Locke and A. D. Booth, Cambridge, Mass. and New York, 1957, pp. 15–23

Machine translation / Translation / Computers / Meaning

205. 1955 WUNDHEILER, Luitgard, and Alex, "Some Logical Concepts for Syntax," *Machine Translation of Languages,* ed. William N. Locke and A. D. Booth, Cambridge, Mass. and New York, 1957, pp. 194–207

Syntax / Logic / Grammar / Meaning

206. 1955 YNGVE, Victor H., "Syntax and the Problem of Multiple Meaning," *Machine Translation of Languages,* ed. William N. Locke and A. D. Booth, Cambridge, Mass. and New York, 1957, pp. 208–226

Machine translation / Syntax / Meaning / Context / German language

206a 1956 CULLER, A. Dwight, "Method in the Study of Victorian Prose," *Victorian Newsletter,* No. 9 (Spring, 1956), 1–4

Rhetoric / English prose, 19C

207. 1956 FUCKS, Wilhelm, *Zur Deutung einfachster mathematischer Sprachcharakteristiken,* Cologne and Opladen, 1956

Quantitative methods / Statistics / Attribution / Aesthetics

208. 1956 HELLENS, Franz (pseud. of Frederic van EMBERGEM), "Style et caractère," *Style et caractère,* Brussels, 1956, pp. 173–188

(Continued)

Expressive theory / Natural style / Impressionism / Definition

*209. 1956 HERDAN, Gustav, *Language as Choice and Chance,* Groningen, 1956
(*See also* No. 266)

Stylostatistics / Quantitative methods / Linguistics / Langue-parole / Survey

210. 1957 CHATMAN, Seymour, "Linguistics, Poetics, and Interpretation: The Phonemic Dimension," *Quarterly Journal of Speech,* XLIII (1957), 248–256
◈
Repr., *Bobbs-Merrill Reprint Series in Language and Linguistics,* No. 13

Poetics / Phonemics / Linguistics / Interpretation

211. 1957 HIGHET, Gilbert, "Tibullus: Style," *Poets in a Landscape,* Harmondsworth, 1959, pp. 156–159

Value / Function words / Translation / Idiosyncratic style

212. 1957 SAYCE, R. A., "Literature and Language," *Essays in Criticism,* VII (1957), 119–133
◈
Repr., *Bobbs-Merrill Reprint Series in Language and Linguistics,* No. 80

Interpretation / Form-content / Wittgenstein / Theory

*213. 1957 SKINNER, B. F., *Verbal Behavior,* New York, 1957

Psychology / Behaviorism / Speech mechanisms / Language

*214. 1958 BOOTH, A. D. "The History and Recent Progress of Machine Translation," *Aspects of Translation,* London, 1958, pp. 88–104

Machine translation / History / Dictionary / Grammar / Problems

*215. 1958 BOOTH, Andrew D., L. BRANDWOOD, and J. P. CLEAVE, *Mechanical Resolution of Linguistic Problems,* London, 1958

Machine translation / Quantitative methods / Computers / Chronology determination / Stylistic analysis / Linguistic problems / German language / French language / Russian language

215a 1958 DOOB, Leonard W., "Behavior and Grammatical Style," *Journal of Abnormal and Social Psychology,* LVI (1958), 398–401

Personality / Idiosyncrasy / Psychology / Quantitative methods

216. 1958 FORSTER, Leonard, "Translation: An Introduction," *Aspects of Translation,* London, 1958, pp. 1–28

Translation / Units / Semantics / Problems / Purposes

217. 1958 MILLER, George A., E. B. NEWMAN, and E. A. FRIEDMAN, "Length-Frequency Statistics for Written English," *Information and Control,* I (1958), 370–389

Word-length / Function words / Information theory / Rank-order

218. 1958 TANCOCK, L. W., "Some Problems of Style in Translation from French," *Aspects of Translation,* London, 1958, pp. 29–51

Translation / French language / Syntax / Idioms / Pitfalls / Problems

219. 1958 YOUNGBLOOD, Joseph E., "Style as Information," *Journal of Music Theory,* II (1958), 24–35

Information theory / Definition / Music / Quantitative methods

220. 1959 COWLEY, Malcolm, *Writers at Work,* New York, 1963

Formation / Writing methods / Forster, E. M. / Faulkner

*221. 1959 GUIRAUD, Pierre, *Problèmes et méthodes de la statistique linguistique,* Dordrecht, 1959

Quantitative methods / Statistics / Vocabulary / Information theory / Phonology / Poetics

222. 1959 HOLLANDER, John, "Versions, Interpretations, and Performances," *On Translation,* ed. Reuben A. Brower, Cambridge, Mass., 1959, pp. 205–231

Translation / Interpretation / Shakespeare

223. 1959 JAKOBSON, Roman, "On Linguistic Aspects of Translation," *On Translation,* ed. Reuben A. Brower, Cambridge, Mass., 1959, pp. 232–239

Translation / Linguistics / Semantics

224. 1959 LA DRIERE, J. Craig, "Literary Form and Form in the Other Arts," *Stil- und Formprobleme in der Literatur,* ed. Paul Böckmann, Heidelberg, 1959, pp. 28–37

Form-content / Meaning / Aesthetics / Poetics / Fine arts

225. 1959 MORIER, Henri, *La psychologie des styles,* Geneva, 1959

Personality / Psychology / Characterology / Typology

226\. 1959 NIDA, Eugene A., "Principles of Translation as Exemplified by Bible Translating," *On Translation,* ed. Reuben A. Brower, Cambridge, Mass., 1959, pp. 11–31

Translation / Bible / Linguistics / Metalinguistics / Semantics

*227. 1959 OETTINGER, Anthony G., "Automatic (Transference, Translation, Remittance, Shunting)," *On Translation,* ed. Reuben A. Brower, Cambridge, Mass., 1959, pp. 240–267

Machine translation / Computers / Programming / Russian language / Vocabulary

228\. 1959 POGGIOLI, Renato, "The Added Artificer," *On Translation,* ed. Reuben A. Brower, Cambridge, Mass., 1959, pp. 137–147

Translation / Aesthetics

229\. 1959 QUINE, Willard V., "Meaning and Translation," *On Translation,* ed. Reuben A. Brower, Cambridge, Mass., 1959, pp. 148–172

Meaning / Semantics / Linguistic philosophy / Logic

230\. 1959 SAVORY, Theodore H., *The Art of Translation,* London, 1959

Translation / History / Translation, methods

231\. 1959 SHERBO, Arthur, "The Uses and Abuses of Internal Evidence," *Bulletin of the New York Public Library,* LXIII (1959), 5–22

Internal evidence / Attribution / Idiosyncratic style / Grammar / Diction

232\. 1959 VERGNAUD, Simone M., "La méthode en stylistique," *Stil- und Formprobleme in der Litera-*

tur, ed. Paul Böckmann, Heidelberg, 1959, pp. 344–351
Poetics / Metrics / Verlaine

233. 1960 CARROLL, John B., "Vectors of Prose Style," *Style in Language,* ed. Thomas A. Sebeok, Cambridge, Mass. and New York, 1960, pp. 283–292
Quantitative methods / Characteristics / Typology

234. 1960 CHATMAN, Seymour, "Comparing Metrical Styles," *Style in Language,* ed. Thomas A. Sebeok, Cambridge, Mass. and New York, 1960, pp. 149–172
Metrics / Poetics / Phonemics / Donne / Pope

235. 1960 HERDAN, Gustav, *Type-Token Mathematics,* The Hague, 1960
Quantitative methods / Statistics / Vocabulary / Type-token ratio / Information theory

236. 1960 HYMES, Dell H., "Phonological Aspects of Style: Some English Sonnets," *Style in Language,* ed. Thomas A. Sebeok, Cambridge, Mass. and New York, 1960, pp. 109–131
Phonology / Poetics / Diction / Keywords / Wordsworth / Keats / Sonnets

237. 1960 LOTZ, John, "Metric Typology," *Style in Language,* ed. Thomas A. Sebeok, Cambridge, Mass. and New York, 1960, pp. 135–148
Metrics / Phonetics

*238. 1960 OSGOOD, Charles E., "Some Effects of Motivation on Style of Encoding," *Style in Language,* ed. Thomas A. Sebeok, Cambridge, Mass. and New York, 1960, pp. 293–306
Psychology / Content analysis

239. 1960 SAPORTA, Sol, "The Application of Linguistics to the Study of Poetic Language," *Style in Language,* ed. Thomas A. Sebeok, Cambridge, Mass. and New York, 1960, pp. 82–93

Poetics / Linguistics / Syntax / Diction

*240. 1960 VINAY, J. P., and J. DARBELNET, *Stylistique comparée du français et de l'anglais,* London and Paris, 1960

Comparative stylistics / Grammar / Rhetoric / Vocabulary / Parts of speech / French-English / Translation

241. 1960 VOEGELIN, C. F., "Casual and Noncasual Utterances within Unified Structure," *Style in Language,* ed. Thomas A. Sebeok, Cambridge, Mass. and New York, 1960, pp. 57–68

Typology / Dialects, rhetorical / Linguistics

242. 1960 WELLS, Rulon, "Nominal and Verbal Style," *Style in Language,* ed. Thomas A. Sebeok, Cambridge, Mass. and New York, 1960, pp. 213–220

Grammar / Parts of speech / Noun-verb ratio / Nominality

243. 1961 BARTH, Gilbert, *Recherches sur la fréquence et la valeur des parties du discours en français, en anglais et en espagnol,* Paris, 1961

Comparative stylistics / Parts of speech / French-English-Spanish / Modern prose

244. 1961 GUIRAUD, Pierre, *La stylistique,* Paris, 1961

Survey / Methods / Theory

245. 1961 GUIRAUD, Pierre, "Pour une sémiologie de l'expression poétique," *Langue et littérature* (Pro-

ceedings of the Eighth Congress, International Federation for Modern Languages and Literatures, Liège, 1960), Paris, 1961, pp. 119–132

Phonetics / Semantics / Poetics

246. 1961 LAMB, Sydney M., "The Digital Computer as an Aid in Linguistics," *Language,* XXXVII (1961), 382–412

◈

Repr., *Bobbs-Merrill Reprint Series in Language and Linguistics,* No. 56

Quantitative methods / Computers / Computational linguistics

*247. 1961 MALBLANC, Alfred, *Stylistique comparée du français et de l'allemand,* Stuttgart, 1961

Comparative stylistics / Vocabulary / Parts of speech / Grammar / Rhetoric / French-German / Translation

248. 1961 PLATH, Warren, "Mathematical Linguistics," *Trends in European and American Linguistics 1930–1960,* ed. C. Mohrmann, A. Sommerfelt and J. Whatmough, Utrecht, 1961, pp. 27–30

Attribution / Quantitative methods / Statistics / Linguistics

249. 1961 RIFFATERRE, Michael, "Vers la définition linguistique du style," *Word,* XVII (1961), 318–344 (Rev. of No. 702)

Survey / Linguistic methods / Theory

250. 1961 SPITZER, Leo, "Les études de style et les différents pays," *Langue et littérature* (Proceedings of the Eighth Congress, International Federation for Modern Languages and Literatures, Liège, 1960), Paris, 1961, pp. 23–38

Survey / Methods

251. 1961 ULLMANN, Stephen, "L'image littéraire: quelques questions de méthode," *Langue et littérature* (Proceedings of the Eighth Congress, International Federation for Modern Languages and Literatures, Liège, 1960), Paris, 1961, pp. 41–59

Imagery / Metaphor / French fiction

*252. 1962 ELLEGÅRD, Alvar, *A Statistical Method for Determining Authorship: The Junius Letters, 1769–1772,* Göteborg, 1962

Attribution / Internal evidence / Quantitative methods / Statistics / Computers / Vocabulary / Junius / English prose, 18C

253. 1962 FRANCIS, W. Nelson, "Syntax and Literary Interpretation," *Report of the Eleventh Annual Round Table Meeting on Linguistics and Language Studies,* ed. Bernard Choseed, Washington, D.C., 1962, pp. 83–92

Syntax / Ambiguity / Thomas, Dylan

*254. 1962 *Freeing the Mind: Articles and Letters from the Times Literary Supplement During March-June 1962,* London, 1962

Information retrieval / Lexicography / Computers / Quantitative methods / Machine translation / Synthetic poetry / Sentence generation

255. 1962 GIBSON, Walker, "The Voice of the Writer," *College Composition and Communication,* XIII (1962), 10–13

Composition / Personality / Individuality

256. 1962 GUIRAUD, Pierre, "Les tendances de la stylistique contemporaine," *Style et littérature,* ed. Pierre Guiraud *et al.,* The Hague, 1962, pp. 11–23

Survey / Rhetoric / Spitzer / Stylo-statistics

257. 1962 HALLIDAY, M. A. K., "Descriptive Linguistics in Literary Studies," *English Studies Today, Third Series,* ed. G. I. Duthie, Edinburgh, 1962, pp. 25–39

◈

Repr., Angus McIntosh and M. A. K. Halliday, *Patterns of Language,* London, 1966, pp. 56–69

Objective methods / Linguistics / Syntax

258. 1962 HERDAN, Gustav, *The Calculus of Linguistic Observations,* The Hague, 1962

Quantitative methods / Statistics / Linguistics / Information theory

*259. 1962 JOOS, Martin, *The Five Clocks,* Bloomington, Ind., 1962

◈

Sel., Dudley Bailey, *Essays on Rhetoric,* New York, 1965, pp. 282–309

Types / Formality / Usage / Levels

*260. 1962 KUFNER, Herbert L., *The Grammatical Structures of English and German,* Chicago, 1962

Contrastive study / Grammar / English-German

261. 1962 LEVIN, Samuel R., *Linguistic Structures in Poetry,* The Hague, 1964

Poetics / Grammar / Linguistics / Shakespeare / Sonnet

262. 1962 LEVIN, Samuel R., "Suprasegmentals and the Performance of Poetry," *Quarterly Journal of Speech,* XLVIII (1962), 366–372

◈

Repr., *Bobbs-Merrill Reprint Series in Language and Linguistics,* No. 1

Poetics / Phonemics / Thomas, Dylan / Speech

*263. 1962 NOWOTTNY, Winifred, *The Language Poets Use,* London, 1962

Poetics / Vocabulary / Metaphor / Symbolism / Semantics

264. 1962 THORNTON, H. and A., *Time and Style,* London, 1962

Temporality / Verb-system / Grammar / Greek language / Latin language / Apposition

264a 1963 ALTICK, Richard D., "Problems of Authorship," *The Art of Literary Research,* New York, 1963, pp. 63–79

Attribution / Internal evidence / Authorship / Canon

265. 1963 BRINEGAR, Claude S., "Mark Twain and the Quintus Curtius Snodgrass Letters: A Statistical Test of Authorship," *Journal of the American Statistical Association,* LVIII (1963), 85–96

Attribution / Word-length / Statistics / Twain

266. 1963 CHRETIEN, C. Douglas, "A New Statistical Approach to the Study of Language," *Romance Philology,* XVI (1963), 290–301
(Rev. of No. 209)

Quantitative methods / Linguistics / Statistics

267. 1963 CHRISTENSEN, Francis, "A New Rhetoric: Sentence Openers," *College English,* XXV (1963), 7–11

Sentence structure / Syntax / Initial constructions / American prose

268. 1963 FRUMKINA, R. M., "The Application of Statistical Methods in Linguistic Research," *Exact Methods in Linguistic Research,* ed. O. S. Akhmanova, *et al.,* Berkeley and Los Angeles, 1963, pp. 80–114

(Continued)

Linguistics / Quantitative methods / Statistics / Information theory

269. 1963 IVES, Sumner, "Grammar and Style," *English Journal,* LII (1963), 364–370

◈

Repr., *Language, Style, Ideas,* ed. Sumner Ives and Stephen O. Mitchell, New York, 1964, pp. 131–142

Grammar / Sentences / Linguistics / Composition

270. 1963 LEVIN, Samuel R., "Deviation—Statistical and Determinate—in Poetic Language," *Lingua,* XII (1963), 276–290

Deviation, linguistic / Poetry / Context / Statistics / Norm, linguistic / Grammaticality / Generative grammar

271. 1963 LEVIN, Samuel R., "On Automatic Production of Poetic Sequences," *Texas Studies in Literature and Language,* V (1963), 138–146

Poetry / Sentence generation / Grammaticality / Computers

*272. 1963 MILES, Josephine, *Eras and Modes in English Poetry,* Berkeley and Los Angeles, 1964

Poetics / English poetry, 19C / Parts of speech / Quantitative methods / Chronology

*273. 1963 MOSTELLER, Frederick, and David L. WALLACE, "Inference in an Authorship Problem," *Journal of the American Statistical Association,* LVIII (1963), 275–309

Quantitative methods / Statistics / Computers / Attribution / *The Federalist*

274. 1963 POSNER, Rebecca, "Linguistique et littérature," *Marche Romane,* XIII (1963), 38–56

Stylistics, definition / Stylistic function / Survey

*274a 1963 POSNER, Rebecca, "The Use and Abuse of Stylistic Statistics," *Archivum Linguisticum*, XV (1963), 111–139

Quantitative methods, criticism / Attribution / Yule / Vocabulary / Keywords

275. 1963 STONE, Philip J., and Earl B. HUNT, "A Computer Approach to Content Analysis: Studies Using the General Inquirer System," *Proceedings, Spring Joint Computer Conference, 1963* (American Federation of Information Processing Societies), Washington, D.C., 1964, pp. 241–256

General Inquirer / Content analysis / Computers / Psychology

276. 1963 TOLLENAERE, F. de, *Nieuwe Wegen in de Lexicologie*, Amsterdam, 1963

Computers / Lexicography / Quantitative methods

277. 1963 *Writers at Work, Second Series*, New York, 1963

Formation / Writing methods / Eliot, T. S. / Hemingway / Huxley / Miller, Henry

278. 1964 DE GROOT, A. Willem, "The Description of a Poem," *Proceedings of the Ninth International Congress of Linguists*, ed. Horace G. Lunt, The Hague, 1964, pp. 294–301

Descriptive poetics / Linguistics / Phonetics

278a 1964 DEHENNIN, E., "La stylistique littéraire en marche," *Revue belge de philologie et d'histoire*, XLII (1964), 880–906

Stylistics, survey / Criticism

278b 1964 DELBOUILLE, Paul, "La méthode des 'champs stylistiques'," *Cahiers d'analyse textuelle,* VI (1964), 81–88

Semantics / Vocabulary / Meaning / French poetry

278c 1964 DELBOUILLE, Paul, "Réflexions sur l'état présent de la stylistique littéraire," *Cahiers d'analyse textuelle,* VI (1964), 5–22

Stylistics, survey / Definition / Objective methods

279. 1964 DUPRIEZ, B., "Jalons pour une stylistique littéraire," *Le français moderne,* XXXII (1964), 45–59

Semantics / Synonyms / Malraux / Spitzer

280. 1964 FOGEL, Ephim, "The Humanist and the Computer: Vision and Actuality," *Literary Data Processing Conference Proceedings,* ed. Jess B. Bessinger, Stephen M. Parrish, and Harry F. Arader, White Plains, N.Y., 1964, pp. 11–24

Computers / Quantitative methods / Shakespeare

281. 1964 HALLIDAY, M. A. K., "The Linguistic Study of Literary Texts," *Proceedings of the Ninth International Congress of Linguists,* ed. Horace G. Lunt, The Hague, 1964, pp. 302–307

Linguistic stylistics / Grammar / Lexicon / Poetics

282. 1964 HERDAN, G., *Quantitative Linguistics,* Washington, D.C., 1964

Quantitative methods / Computational linguistics / Statistics / Vocabulary / Comparative stylistics

283. 1964 MARKMAN, Alan, "Litterae ex Machina," *Literary Data Processing Conference Proceedings,*

ed. Jess B. Bessinger, Stephen M. Parrish, and Harry F. Arader, White Plains, N.Y., 1964, pp. 37–54

Computers / Content analysis / Medieval literature

*284. 1964 MOSTELLER, Frederick, and David L. WALLACE, *Inference and Disputed Authorship: The Federalist,* Reading, Mass., 1964

Quantitative methods / Statistics / Computers / Attribution / *The Federalist*

*285. 1964 OHMANN, Richard, "Generative Grammars and the Concept of Literary Style," *Word,* XX (1964), 423–439

Definition / Survey / Generative grammar / Syntax / Faulkner / Hemingway

286. 1964 PAISLEY, William J., "Identifying the Unknown Communicator in Painting, Literature and Music: The Significance of Minor Encoding Habits," *The Journal of Communication,* XIV (1964), 219–237

Attribution / Internal evidence / Aesthetics / Music

287. 1964 RABEN, Joseph, "A Computer-Aided Study of Literary Influence: Milton to Shelley," *Literary Data Processing Conference Proceedings,* ed. Jess B. Bessinger, Stephen M. Parrish, and Harry F. Arader, White Plains, N.Y., 1964, pp. 230–274

Computers / Quantitative methods / Word index / Poetry / Influence / Milton / Shelley

288. 1964 RIFFATERRE, Michael, "L'étude stylistique des formes littéraires conventionelles," *French Review,* XXXVIII (1964), 3–14

Affectivity / Context / Stylistic devices / Conventional phrases

289. 1964 RIFFATERRE, Michael, "Fonctions du cliché dans la prose littéraire," *Cahiers de l'association internationale des études françaises,* No. 16 (March 1964), 81–95

Cliché / Stylistic devices / Context

290. 1964 SEDELOW, Sally Yeates, and Walter A., *A Preface to Computational Stylistics,* Santa Monica, Calif., 1964

◈

Repr. *The Computer and Literary Style,* ed. Jacob Leed, Kent, Ohio, 1966, pp. 1–13

Computational stylistics / Survey / Computers

291. 1964 SEDELOW, Sally Yeates, Walter A. SEDELOW, Jr., and Terry RUGGLES, "Some Parameters for Computational Stylistics: Computer Aids to the Use of Traditional Categories in Stylistic Analysis," *Literary Data Processing Conference Proceedings,* ed. Jess B. Bessinger, Stephen M. Parrish, and Harry F. Arader, White Plains, N.Y., 1964, pp. 211–229

Quantitative methods / Computers / Content analysis / Survey / Computational stylistics

292. 1964 SPENCER, John, and Michael J. GREGORY, "An Approach to the Study of Style," *Linguistics and Style,* ed. John Spencer, London, 1964, pp. 59–105

Linguistic stylistics / Methods

293. 1965 ALLPORT, Gordon W., *Letters from Jenny,* New York, 1965

Personality / Content analysis / Traits / Style of life / Psychology

294. 1965 GLINZ, Hans, "The Relation Between Inner and Outer Form," *Report of the Sixteenth Annual Round Table Meeting on Linguistics and Language Studies,* ed. Charles W. Kreidler, Washington, D.C., 1965, pp. 19–26

Semantics / Linguistics / Syntax / Lexicon

295. 1965 LEECH, Geoffrey, " 'This bread I break'—Language and Interpretation," *Review of English Literature,* VI (1965), 66–75

Deviation, linguistic / Thomas, Dylan / Poetry / Interpretation / Meaning

296. 1965 MILLER, Henry Knight, "Internal Evidence: Professor Sherbo and the Case of Arthur Murphy," *Bulletin of the New York Public Library,* LXIX (1965), 459–470

Internal evidence / Attribution / Murphy, Arthur / Parallels, verbal

297. 1965 SHERBO, Arthur, "Imitation or Concealment: Who Wrote the *Entertainer* Essays?" *Bulletin of the New York Public Library,* LXIX (1965), 471–486

Internal evidence / Attribution / Murphy, Arthur / Parallels, verbal

297a 1966 FOWLER, Roger, "Linguistics, Stylistics; Criticism?" *Lingua,* XVI (1966), 153–165

Linguistics / Generative grammar / Criticism / Levels / Context / Definition / Survey

297b 1966 COHEN, Jean, *Structure du language poétique,* Paris, 1966

Poetics / Quantitative methods / Adjectives / Epithets / Word-order / Inversion / French poetry, 17C, 19C

297c 1966 LEVISON, M., A. Q. MORTON, and W. C. WAKE, "On Certain Statistical Features of the Pauline Epistles," *Philosophical Journal,* III (1966), 129–148

Quantitative methods / Statistics / Sentence-length / Conjunctions / Attribution / St. Paul

298. 1966 MILIC, Louis T., "Metaphysics in the Criticism of Style," *College Composition and Communication,* XVII (1966), 124–129

◈

Repr., *New Rhetorics,* ed. Martin Steinmann, Jr., New York, 1967, pp. 161–175

Impressionism / Objective methods

298a 1966 OHMANN, Richard, "Literature as Sentences," *College English,* XXVII (1966), 261–267

Linguistic method / Generative grammar / Sentences / Grammaticalness / Deep structure

298b 1966 SCHOENBAUM, S., *Internal Evidence and Elizabethan Dramatic Authorship,* Evanston, Ill., 1966

Attribution / Internal evidence / English drama, 16–17C / Survey

299. 1966 SOMERS, H. H., "Statistical Methods in Literary Analysis," *The Computer and Literary Style,* ed. Jacob Leed, Kent, Ohio, 1966, pp. 128–140

Attribution / Quantitative methods / Statistics, non-parametric / Adjective-verb quotient / St. Paul

300. 1966 WACHAL, Robert S., "On Using a Computer," *The Computer and Literary Style,* ed. Jacob Leed, Kent, Ohio, 1966, pp. 14–37

Computers / Quantitative methods, introduction

300a. 1967 COQUET, J. C., "L'objet stylistique," *Le français moderne,* XXXV (1967), 53–67

Linguistic methods / Information theory / Expressivity / Spitzer

Part Three

APPLIED

*301. 1710 SWIFT, Jonathan, *The Tatler,* No. CCXXX, *Bickerstaff Papers and Pamphlets on the Church,* ed. Herbert Davis, Oxford, 1940, pp. 173–177

English prose, 18C / Reform / Vocabulary / Slang

*302. 1712 SWIFT, Jonathan, "A Proposal for Correcting, Improving and Ascertaining the English Tongue," *A Proposal for Correcting the English Tongue, Polite Conversation, Etc.,* ed. Herbert Davis with Louis Landa, Oxford, 1957, pp. 5–21

English language / Reform / Purism / Academy / Deterioration

*303. 1721 SWIFT, Jonathan, "A Letter to a Young Gentleman, Lately Entered into Holy Orders," *Irish*

Tracts and Sermons, ed. Herbert Davis, Oxford, 1948, pp. 61–81

English prose, 18C / Sermon / Vocabulary / Reform

304. 1726 MATHER, Cotton, "Of Poetry and Style," *Manuductio ad Ministerium,* Boston, 1726

◈

Repr., *The Puritans,* ed. Perry Miller and Thomas H. Johnson, New York, 1963, Vol. II, pp. 684–689

English prose, 18C / Sermon / Ars dicendi / Ciceronian-Senecan / Personality / Plain style

305. 1745 BYLES, Mather, "Bombastic and Grubstreet Style: A Satire," *The American Magazine and Historical Chronicle,* Jan. 1745, pp. 1–4

◈

Repr., *The Puritans,* ed. Perry Miller and Thomas H. Johnson, New York, 1963, Vol. II, pp. 689–694

American prose, 18C / Bombastic style / Reform

306. 1818 COLERIDGE, Samuel Taylor, "Lecture XIV: On Style," *Literary Remains,* ed. H. N. Coleridge, 2 v., London, 1836

◈

Repr., Lane Cooper, *Theories of Style,* New York, 1907, pp. 199–208

English prose, 17–19C / Deterioration / Ars dicendi

307. 1861 ARNOLD, Matthew, "On Translating Homer," *On the Classical Tradition,* ed. R. H. Super, Ann Arbor, Mich., 1960, pp. 97–168

Translation / Homer / Greek language / Grand style / Pope / Plain style / Simplicity

307a 1870 ABBOTT, E. A., *A Shakespearian Grammar,* New York, 1966

English language, 16C / Shakespeare / Syntax / Morphology / Parts of speech / Idiom / Vocabulary / Functional shift / Imagery / Prosody

308. 1870 WHITE, Richard Grant, "Styles of Disraeli and Dickens," *Galaxy,* X (1870), 253–263
English fiction, 19C / Disraeli / Dickens / Diction / Idiom / Errors

309. 1876 SAINTSBURY, George, "Modern English Prose," *Collected Essays and Papers,* London, 1923, Vol. III, pp. 62–87
English prose, 19C / Deterioration / Value / Cliché / Aristocracy / Ruskin / Arnold / Pater / Sentence

310. 1885 SAINTSBURY, George, "English Prose Style," *Collected Essays and Papers,* London, 1923, Vol. III, pp. 88–119
English prose, history / Vernacularity / Ornament / Poetic style / Typology / Plain style / Flamboyant style / Prose rhythm

*311. 1888 SHERMAN, Lucius A., "Some Observations upon the Sentence Lengths in English Prose," *University of Nebraska Studies,* I (1888), 119–130
English prose / Quantitative methods / Sentence-length

312. 1892 COOK, Albert S., *The Bible and English Prose Style,* Boston, 1892
English prose, 17C/ Biblical prose / Translation / Bible

313. 1894 GERWIG, George William, "On the Decrease of Predication and of Sentence Weight in English Prose," *University of Nebraska Studies,* II (1894), 17–44
English prose / Sentences / Grammar / Verbs / Quantitative methods

314. 1894 LEWIS, Edwin Herbert, *The History of the English Paragraph,* Chicago, 1894

English language / Paragraph / Sentence-length / Connection

315. 1895 TWAIN, Mark, "Fenimore Cooper's Literary Offenses," *North American Review,* CLXI (1895), 1–12

◈

Repr., *Bobbs-Merrill Reprint Series in Language and Linguistics,* No. 90

American fiction, 19C / Cooper, Fenimore / Errors / Bad style / Diction

316. 1896 BREWSTER, William Tenney, *Studies in Structure and Style,* New York, 1911

English prose, 19C / Stevenson / Morley / Froude / Arnold / Ruskin / Newman / Diction / Syntax / Rhetoric / Models

317. c.1896 TWAIN, Mark, "Fenimore Cooper's Further Literary Offenses," ed. Bernard De Voto, *New England Quarterly,* XIX (1946), 291–301

◈

Repr., "Cooper's Prose Style," *Letters from the Earth,* ed. Bernard De Voto, New York, 1962, pp. 137–145

American fiction, 19C / Cooper, Fenimore / Errors / Bad style

318. 1897 HILDRETH, Carson, "The Bacon-Shakespeare Controversy; a Contribution," *University of Nebraska Studies,* II (1897), 147–162

Shakespeare question / Attribution / Sentence length / Quantitative methods

319. 1900 MEYNELL, Alice, "A Corrupt Following," *The Second Person Singular,* Oxford, 1922, pp. 42–48
◈
Repr., *The Character of Prose,* ed. Wallace Douglas, Boston, 1959, pp. 1063–1066

English prose, 18C / Gibbon / Correctness / Deterioration / Errors, grammatical / Influence

320. 1903 MEYNELL, Alice, "Charles Dickens as a Man of Letters," *Atlantic Monthly,* XCI (1903), 52–59

English prose, 19C / Dickens / Vocabulary / Macaulay / Influence

321. 1905 GOURMONT, Remy de, "Le style et l'art de Stendhal," *Promenades littéraires,* II, Paris, 1963, pp. 78–84

French fiction, 19C / Stendhal / Plain style

321a 1905 JESPERSEN, Otto, *Growth and Structure of the English Language,* 9th ed., Oxford, 1945

English language, inventory / Vocabulary / Latinism / Grammar / Poetic language / Shakespeare

321b 1907 UHRSTROM, Wilhelm, *Studies on the Language of Samuel Richardson,* Upsala, 1907

English fiction, 18C / Richardson / Grammar / Inflection / Parts of speech / Syntax / Vocabulary

322. 1908 LANSON, Gustave, *L'art de la prose,* Paris, 1908

French prose, history / Impressionism / Genre

*323. 1909 BALLY, Charles, *Traité de stylistique française,* 2 v., Heidelberg, 1909

French language, inventory / Theory / Methods / Vocabulary / Etymology / Rhetorical devices / Affectivity / Figurative language / Social dialects

324. 1912 SAINTSBURY, George, *A History of English Prose Rhythm,* London, 1912

English prose, history / Prose rhythm / Metrics

325. 1913 VOSSLER, Karl, *Langue et culture de la France,* tr. Alphonse Juilland, Paris, 1953

French language / National character / Idealism

326. 1914 CROLL, Morris W., "Juste Lipse et le mouvement anti-cicéronien," *Revue du seizième siècle,* II (1914), 200–242

◈

Repr., *Style, Rhetoric, and Rhythm: Essays by Morris W. Croll,* ed. J. Max Patrick *et al.,* Princeton, 1966, pp. 7–44

Rhetoric, Renaissance / Latin prose, 16C / Lipsius / Anti-Ciceronian style

327. 1914 HORTEN, Franz, *Studien über die Sprache Defoes,* Bonn, 1914

English prose, 18C / Defoe / Pure style / Spelling / Saxonism / Englishness / Function words / Word order / Verbs / Sentence structure

328. 1914 THIBAUDET, Albert, "La critique et le style," *Réflexions sur la critique,* Paris, 1939, pp. 58–71

French fiction, 19C / Flaubert / Consciousness / Personality / Multiple styles / Formation

*329. 1915 KRAPP, George Philip, *The Rise of English Literary Prose,* New York, 1963

English prose, 14–16C / English language / Wyclif / Bacon / Bible / Sermon

*330. 1916 CROLL, Morris W., and Harry CLEMONS, "The Sources of the Euphuistic Rhetoric," *Euphues: The Anatomy of Wit; Euphues and His England by John Lyly,* ed. Morris W. Croll and Harry Clemons, New York, 1964, pp. xv–lxiv

◈

Repr., *Style, Rhetoric, and Rhythm: Essays by Morris W. Croll,* ed. J. Max Patrick, *et al.,* Princeton, 1966, pp. 241–295

English prose, 16C / Lyly / Rhetoric, Renaissance / Euphuism

*331. 1916 QUILLER-COUCH, Sir Arthur, *The Art of Writing,* New York, 1961

English prose, 19C / Prose-verse / Ars dicendi / Diction

332. 1918 HARKNESS, Stanley, "The Prose Style of Sir Philip Sidney," *University of Washington Studies in Language and Literature,* No. 2, Madison, Wis., 1918, pp. 57–76

English prose, 16C / Sidney / Sentence length / Sentence structure / Errors / Prose rhythm

333. 1918 HERFORD, C. H., "English Prose Numbers," *Essays and Studies by Members of the English Association,* IV (1918), 29–54

English prose / Rhythm / Meter / Cadence / Quantitative methods

334. 1918 TAYLOR, Warner, "The Prose Style of Johnson," *University of Wisconsin Studies in Language and Literature,* 2, Madison, Wis., 1918, pp. 22–56

(Continued)

English prose, 18C / Johnson / Quantitative methods / Word-length / Sentence-length / Periodic sentence / Parallelism

335. 1919 CROLL, Morris W., "The Cadence of English Oratorical Prose," *Studies in Philology,* XVI (1919), 1–55

◈

Repr., *Style, Rhetoric, and Rhythm: Essays by Morris W. Croll,* ed. J. Max Patrick, *et al.,* Princeton, 1966, pp. 303–359

English prose, 16C / Book of Common Prayer / Prose rhythm / Metrics / Cadence

336. 1919 THIBAUDET, Albert, "Sur le style de Flaubert," *Nouvelle revue française,* XIII (1919), 942–953

◈

Repr., *Réflexions sur la critique,* Paris, 1939, pp. 72–81

(*See also* Nos. 338, 340)

French fiction, 19C / Flaubert / Grammar / Errors / Formation

337. 1920 HALE, William Bayard, *The Story of a Style,* New York, 1920

American prose, 20C / Wilson, Woodrow / Pleonasm / Doublets / Political style

*338. 1920 PROUST, Marcel, "A propos du 'style' de Flaubert," *Nouvelle revue française,* XIV (1920), 72–90

◈

Repr., *Chroniques,* Paris, 1949, pp. 193–211

(*See also* Nos. 336, 340)

French fiction, 19C / Flaubert / Grammar / Verb / Imagery

339. 1920 SAMPSON, George, "On Playing the Sedulous Ape," *Essays and Studies by Members of the English Association,* VI (1920), 67–87

English prose, 19C / Stevenson / Imitation / Models / Formation / Impressionism

340. 1920 THIBAUDET, Albert, "Lettre à M. Marcel Proust," *Nouvelle revue française,* XIV (1920), 426–441
◈
Repr., *Réflexions sur la critique,* Paris, 1939, pp. 82–97
(*See also* Nos. 336, 338)

French fiction, 19C / Flaubert / Grammar / Syntax / Innovation

*341. 1921 CROLL, Morris W., "Attic Prose in the Seventeenth Century," *Studies in Philology,* XVIII (1921), 79–128
◈
Repr., *Style, Rhetoric, and Rhythm: Essays by Morris W. Croll,* ed. J. Max Patrick, *et al.,* Princeton, 1966, pp. 51–101

English prose, 17C / Rhetoric, Classical / Attic prose / Anti-Ciceronian / Levels / Plain style

342. 1922 BARNES, Matthew, "What is Pure French?" *Society for Pure English Tract No. VIII,* Oxford, 1922

French language / Gourmont / Vocabulary / Purism

343. 1923 ARONSTEIN, Philipp, *Englische Stilistik,* 2d ed., Leipzig, 1926

English language, inventory / Devices, stylistic / Parts of speech / Sentence structure / Word order / Rhetoric

344. 1923 AURNER, Robert R., "Caxton and the English Sentence," *Wisconsin Studies in Language and Literature*, XVIII (1923), 23–59

English prose / Caxton / Sentences / Connectives

345. 1923 AURNER, Robert R., "The History of Certain Aspects of the Structure of the English Sentence," *Philological Quarterly*, II (1923), 187–208

English prose / Sentence structure / Sentence-length / Connectives

346. 1923 CROLL, Morris W., "Attic Prose: Lipsius, Montaigne, Bacon," *Schelling Anniversary Papers*, New York, 1923, pp. 117–151

◈

Repr., *Style, Rhetoric, and Rhythm: Essays by Morris W. Croll*, ed. J. Max Patrick, *et al.*, Princeton, 1966, pp. 167–206

English prose, 17C / French prose, 16C / Latin prose, Renaissance / Lipsius / Montaigne / Bacon / Attic prose / Anti-Ciceronian / Rhetoric

347. 1923 LEE, Vernon (pseud. of Violet PAGET), *The Handling of Words and Other Studies in Literary Psychology*, London, 1923

English prose, 19C / De Quincey / Landor / Carlyle / Meredith / Kipling / Stevenson / Hardy / James / Syntax / Verbs / Tenses / Numerical methods

348. 1924 CROLL, Morris W., "Muret and the History of 'Attic' Prose," *PMLA*, XXXIX (1924), 245–309

◈

Repr., *Style, Rhetoric, and Rhythm: Essays by Morris W. Croll*, ed. J. Max Patrick, *et al.*, Princeton, 1966, pp. 107–162

Latin prose, 16C / Muret / Attic prose / Anti-Ciceronian / Vernacular / Rhetoric

349. 1924 HARVITT, Hélène, "How Henry James revised *Roderick Hudson:* A Study in Style," *PMLA,* XXXIX (1924), 203–227

American prose, 19C / James, Henry / Revision / Chronology

350. 1924 HOLMES, Elizabeth, "Some Notes on Milton's Use of Words," *Essays and Studies by Members of the English Association,* X (1924), 97–121

English poetry, 17C/ Milton / Diction / Etymology / Latinism / Concreteness

351. 1925 KRAPP, George Philip, "Style," *The English Language in America,* New York, 1925, Vol. I, pp. 274–327

American prose / Slang / Folk style /Literary prose / Oratory / Diction

352. 1926 ELIOT, T. S., "For Lancelot Andrewes," *Selected Essays: 1917–1932,* New York, 1947, pp. 289–300

English prose, 17C / Andrewes, Lancelot / Donne / Sermon / Diction

353. 1926 SPITZER, Leo, "Zum Stil Marcel Prousts," *Stilstudien,* 2d ed., Munich, 1961, Vol. II, pp. 365–497

French fiction, 20C /Proust / Prose rhythm / Sentence structure / Verb / Connection / Duration

354. 1927 CRANE, Ronald S., "Introduction," *New Essays by Oliver Goldsmith,* ed. Ronald S. Crane, Chicago, 1927, pp. xi–xli

English prose, 18C / Goldsmith / Attribution / Idea-repetition

*355. 1928 CHANDLER, Zilpha Emma, *An Analysis of the Stylistic Techniques of Addison, Johnson, Hazlitt and Pater,* Iowa City, 1928

English prose, 18–19C / Johnson / Addison / Hazlitt / Pater / Diction / Syntax / Imagery / Rhetoric / Sentence-length

356. 1928 GORDON, George, "Shakespeare's English," *Society for Pure English Tract No. XXIX,* Oxford, 1928

English language, 16C/ Shakespeare / Diction / Dialect

357. 1928 ZEITLIN, Jacob, "The Development of Bacon's Essays," *Journal of English and Germanic Philology,* XXVII (1928), 496–519

English prose, 17C / Bacon / Development / Senecan-Ciceronian / Alteration

*358. 1929 CROLL, Morris W., "The Baroque Style in Prose," *Studies in English Philology: A Miscellany in Honor of Frederick Klaeber,* ed. Kemp Malone and Martin B. Ruud, Minneapolis, 1929, pp. 427–456 ◈

Repr., *Style, Rhetoric, and Rhythm: Essays by Morris W. Croll,* ed. J. Max Patrick, *et al.,* Princeton, 1966, pp. 207–233

English prose, 17C / Baroque style / Curt style / Loose style / Sentence structure / Punctuation

359. 1929 FRIES, Charles C., "One Stylistic Feature of the 1611 English Bible," *The Fred Newton Scott Anniversary Papers,* Chicago, 1929, pp. 175–187

English prose, 17C / Bible / Translation / Influence / Parts of speech / Adjectives / Contrastive / Greek-English / Concreteness / Simplicity

360. 1929 HAZARD, Paul, "Le style de *Manon Lescaut*," *Etudes critiques sur Manon Lescaut*, Chicago, 1929, pp. 71–83

French fiction, 18C / Prévost / Natural style

*361. 1929 LEONARD, Sterling A., *The Doctrine of Correctness in English Usage: 1700–1800*, New York, 1962

English prose, 18C /Purism / Diction / Errors / Grammar / Usage / Correctness

*362. 1930 JONES, Richard F., "Science and English Prose Style in the Third Quarter of the Seventeenth Century," *PMLA*, XLV (1930), 977–1009

◈ Repr., *The Seventeenth Century*, Stanford, 1951, pp. 75–110

English prose, 17C / Scientific prose / Royal Society / Plain style

363. 1930 MAYO, T. F., "The Authorship of the History of John Bull," *PMLA*, XLV (1930), 274–282

English prose, 18C / Arbuthnot / Swift / Attribution / Internal evidence / Characteristic words and phrases

*364. 1931 JONES, Richard F., "The Attack on Pulpit Eloquence in the Restoration," *Journal of English and Germanic Philology*, XXX (1931), 188–217

◈ Repr., *The Seventeenth Century*, Stanford, 1951, pp. 111–142

English prose, 17C / Enthusiastic style / Plain style / Scientific prose / Royal Society

365. 1931 TAYLOR, Archer, "The Style of Proverbs," *The Proverb and Index*, Hatboro, Penna., 1962, pp. 135–183

Proverbs / Folk style

*366. 1932 CHAMBERS, R. W., "The Continuity of English Prose from Alfred to More and His School," *Nicholas Harpsfield's The Life and Death of Sir Thomas Moore, Knight . . .* , ed. Elsie Vaughan Hitchcock (Early English Text Society), London, 1932, pp. xlv–clxxiv

English prose, early history / More / Influence / Religious prose

*367. 1932 JONES, Richard F., "Science and Language in England of the Mid-Seventeenth Century," *Journal of English and Germanic Philology,* XXXI (1932), 315–331

◈

Repr., *The Seventeenth Century,* Stanford, 1951, pp. 143–160

English prose, 17C / Words-things / Plain style / Bacon / Universal language / Scientific prose

368. 1932 MITCHELL, W. Fraser, *English Pulpit Oratory from Andrewes to Tillotson,* New York, 1962

English prose, 17C / Sermon / Reform / Rhetoric / Andrewes / Donne / Taylor / Tillotson / Restoration prose

369. 1933 REYNOLDS, W. V., "Johnson's Opinions on Prose Style," *Review of English Studies,* IX (1933), 433–446

English prose, 18C / Johnson / Ideals, 18C / Ars dicendi

*370. 1933 WILLIAMSON, George, "The Restoration Revolt against Enthusiasm," *Studies in Philology,* XXX (1933), 571–603

◈

Repr., *Seventeenth Century Contexts,* London, 1960, pp. 202–239

English prose, 17C / Dryden / Plain style / Enthusiastic style

*371. 1934 BATESON, F. W., *English Poetry and the English Language,* Oxford, 1934

English poetry, history / Theory of language, history / Reflection theory

*372. 1934 DOBREE, Bonamy, *Modern Prose Style,* 2d ed., Oxford, 1964

◈
Sel., Paul C. Wermuth, *Modern Essays on Writing and Style,* New York, 1964, pp. 140–154

English prose, 20C / Personality / Types / Modern prose

373. 1935 FORT, Joseph-Barthélémy, *Samuel Butler l'écrivain: étude d'un style,* Bordeaux, 1935

English fiction, 19C / Butler, Samuel / Diction / Imagery / Ideals / Types

374. 1935 REYNOLDS, W. V., "The Reception of Johnson's Prose Style," *Review of English Studies,* XI (1935), 145–162

English prose, 18C / Johnson / Ideals, 18C

*375. 1935 SPURGEON, Caroline F. E., *Shakespeare's Imagery,* Boston, 1961

English drama, 16–17C / Shakespeare / Imagery / Personality

376. 1936 DELCOURT, J., "Some Aspects of Thomas More's English," *Essays and Studies by Members of the English Association,* XXI (1936), 7–31

English prose, 16C / More / Syntax / Innovation / Modernity / Vocabulary / Figurative language / Popular language

377. 1936 RUNION, Howard L., "An Objective Study of the Speech Style of Woodrow Wilson," *Speech Monographs,* III (1936), 75–94

American prose, 20C / Wilson, Woodrow / Speech style / Objective methods

378. 1936 SMITH, Logan Pearsall, "Fine Writing," *Society for Pure English Tract No. XLVI,* Oxford, 1936

◈

Repr., Paul C. Wermuth, *Modern Essays on Writing and Style,* New York, 1964, pp. 222–232

English language, 20C / Composition / Rhetoric / Theory / Fine writing

379. 1936 SMITH, Logan Pearsall, "Thomas Carlyle: The Rembrandt of English Prose," *Reperusals and Re-Collections,* London, 1936

◈

Repr., *Victorian Literature: Modern Essays in Criticism,* ed. Austin Wright, New York, 1961, pp. 113–127

English prose, 19C / Carlyle / Development / Vocabulary / Expressiveness

*380. 1936 WILLIAMSON, George, "Senecan Style in the Seventeenth Century," *Philological Quarterly,* XV (1936), 321–351

English prose, 17C / Senecan style

381. 1936 WILLIAMSON, George, "Strong Lines," *English Studies,* XVIII (1936), 152–159

◈

Repr., *Seventeenth Century Contexts,* London, 1960, pp. 120–131

English poetry, 17C / Strong lines / Conceits / Metaphysical poetry

382. 1937 CRANE, W. G., *Wit and Rhetoric in the Renaissance: The Formal Basis of Elizabethan Prose Style,* New York, 1937

◈

Sel., Joseph Schwartz and John A. Rycenga, *The Province of Rhetoric,* New York, 1965, pp. 275–292, 311–329

English prose, 16C / School rhetoric / Renaissance rhetoric / Theory

383. 1937 TILLOTSON, Geoffrey, "Elizabethan Decoration," *Essays in Criticism and Research,* Cambridge, 1942, pp. 5–16

Rhetoric, Elizabethan / Aesthetics / Imagery / Decoration

*384. 1938 CONNOLLY, Cyril, "Predicament," *Enemies of Promise,* Harmondsworth, 1961, pp. 15–94

◈

Sel., Paul C. Wermuth, *Modern Essays on Writing and Style,* New York, 1964

English prose, 20C / Mandarin style / Plain style

385. 1938 MAPES, E. K., "Implications of Some Recent Studies on Style," *Revue de littérature comparée,* XVIII (1938), 514–533

French poetry, 19C / Hugo / Adjectivals / Epithets

386. 1938 TILLYARD, E. M. W., "A Note on Milton's Style," *The Miltonic Setting,* London, 1957, pp. 105–140

English poetry, 17C / Milton / Diction / Syntax / Latinism / Grand style

387. 1939 BOUGHNER, Daniel C., "Notes on Hooker's Prose," *Review of English Studies,* XV (1939), 194–200

English prose, 16C / Hooker / Prose rhythm / Oral style / Figures / Connection / Rhetorical analysis

388. 1939 FRANÇOIS, Alexis, "Précurseurs français de la grammaire 'affective'," *Mélanges de linguistique offerts à Charles Bally,* Geneva, 1939, pp. 369–377

French language / Grammar / Affectivity

389. 1939 GROOM, Bernard, "On the Diction of Tennyson, Browning and Arnold," *Society for Pure English Tract No. LIII,* Oxford, 1939

English prose, 19C / Tennyson / Browning / Arnold / Diction

390. 1939 LASCELLES, Mary, "Style," *Jane Austen and Her Art,* London, 1958, pp. 87–116

English fiction, 19C /Austen / Rhetoric / Syntax / Diction / Imagery

391. 1939 NEUMANN, Joshua H., "Notes on Ben Jonson's English," *PMLA,* LIV (1939), 736–763

English prose, 17C / Jonson / Vocabulary / Latinism / Modernity / Dialect / Word-borrowing / Coinage / Inkhorn terms / Authority / Ideals

392. 1940 HALLER, Elisabeth, *Die barocken Stilmerkmale in der englischen lateinischen und deutschen Fassung von Dr. Thomas Burnets "Theory of the Earth,"* Zofingen, n.d.

English prose, 17C / Burnet, Thomas / Baroque style / Contrastive study / Sentences / Doublets / Connection / Imagery

393. 1940 LUMIANSKY, R. M., "Milton's English Again," *Modern Language Notes,* LV (1940), 591–594

English poetry, 17C / Milton / Vocabulary / Native-Romance ratio

*394. 1940 MAYER, Gilbert, *La qualification affective dans les romans d'Honoré de Balzac,* Paris, 1940

French fiction, 19C / Balzac / Modification / Adjectives / Seriation / Epithets

395. 1940 MERITT, Herbert, "The Vocabulary of Sir John Cheke's Partial Version of the Gospels," *Journal of English and Germanic Philology,* XXXIX (1940), 450–455

English prose, 16C / Cheke / Bible / Translation / Vocabulary / Saxonism

396. 1940 WORKMAN, S. K., *Fifteenth Century Translation as an Influence on English Prose,* Princeton, 1940

English prose, 15C / Translation / Sentence structure

397. 1940 ZICKGRAF, Gertraut, *Swifts Stilforderungen und Stil,* Marburg, 1940

English prose, 18C / Swift / Ideals / Parts of speech / Sentence / Diction

398. 1941 BEACH, Joseph Warren, "Style in *For Whom the Bell Tolls,*" *American Fiction, 1920–1940,* New York, 1941, pp. 111–119

◈

Repr., *Ernest Hemingway,* ed. Carlos Baker, New York, 1962, pp. 82–86

American fiction, 20C / Hemingway / Spanish idiom / Diction

399. 1941 BECK, Warren, "William Faulkner's Style," *American Prefaces,* Spring 1941, 195–211

◈

Repr., *William Faulkner: Two Decades of Criticism,* ed. Frederick J. Hoffman and Olga W. Vickery, East Lansing, Mich., 1951, pp. 147–164

American fiction, 20C / Faulkner / Diction / Colloquialism / Sentence structure / Imagery

400. 1941 BENNETT, Joan, "An Aspect of the Evolution of Seventeenth-Century Prose," *Review of English Studies,* XVII (1941), 281–297

English prose, 17C / Sermons / Metaphor / Imagery

401. 1941 CRESSOT, M., "La liaison des phrases dans *Salammbô,*" *Le français moderne,* IX (1941), 81–93

French fiction, 19C / Flaubert / Connectives / Grammar / Sentence structure

*402. 1941 MAROUZEAU, J., *Précis de stylistique française,* 4th ed., Paris, 1959

French language / Stylistic inventory

403. 1941 ROSS, John F., *Swift and Defoe,* Berkeley and Los Angeles, 1941

English prose, 18C / Defoe / Swift / Comparative study / Irony / Syntax

404. 1941 ROUSE, W. H. D., "Style," *Essays and Studies by Members of the English Association,* XXVII (1941), Oxford, 1942, 52–65

◈

Sel., Paul C. Wermuth, *Modern Essays on Writing and Style,* New York, 1964, pp. 181–191

Parody / Versions / Gibbon / Carlyle / Macaulay / James, Henry

405. 1941 SCHORER, Mark, "The Background of a Style," *Kenyon Review,* III (1941), 101–105

◈

Repr., *Ernest Hemingway,* ed. Carlos Baker, New York, 1962, pp. 87–89

American fiction, 20C / Hemingway / Multiple styles / Sentence structure

406. 1941 STEEL, Eric M., *Diderot's Imagery: A Study of a Literary Personality,* New York, 1941

French prose, 18C /Diderot / Imagery / Personality / Psychology

*407. 1941 WIMSATT, W. K., Jr., *The Prose Style of Samuel Johnson,* New Haven, 1963

◈

Sel., *Essays in the Language of Literature,* ed. Seymour Chatman and S. R. Levin, Boston, 1967, pp. 362–373

English prose, 18C / Johnson / Rhetoric / Diction / Imitation / Ideals

408. 1942 GUICHARD, Léon, "L'écrivain," *Sept études sur Marcel Proust,* Cairo, 1942, pp. 277–320

French fiction, 20C / Proust / Originality / Correctness / Sentence structure / Metaphor

409. 1942 JONES, R. F., "The Moral Sense of Simplicity," *Studies in Honor of Frederick W. Shipley,* St. Louis, 1942, pp. 265–287

English prose, 17C / Moral simplicity / Eloquence / Plain style / Puritan style / Science / Translation / Ideals

410. 1942 LEWIS, C. S., "The Style of Secondary Epic," *A Preface to Paradise Lost,* Oxford, 1959, pp. 39–50

English poetry / Milton / Epic style / Grand style

411. 1942 MAYS, Morley J., "Johnson and Blair on Addison's Prose Style," *Studies in Philology,* XXXIX (1942), 638–649

English prose, 18C / Johnson / Blair / Addison / Middle style / Ideals, 18C / Types

412. 1942 MILES, Josephine, *Wordsworth and the Vocabulary of Emotion,* New York, 1965

English poetry, 19C / Wordsworth / Vocabulary / Meaning / Context / Quantitative methods

*413. 1942 TILLOTSON, Geoffrey, "Eighteenth-Century Poetic Diction," *Essays in Criticism and Research,* London, 1942

◈

Repr., "Augustan Poetic Diction: I and II," *Augustan Studies,* London, 1961, pp. 13–110

English poetry, 18C / Pope / Diction

413a 1942 WIMSATT, W. K., Jr., "When Is Variation 'Elegant'?" *College English,* III (1942), 368–383

◈

Repr., *The Verbal Icon,* New York, 1960, pp. 187–199
(*See* No. 100)

English language, 20C / Rhetorical devices / Repetition / Variation / Errors / Bad style

414. 1943 BISCHOFF, Dietrich, *Sir Thomas Browne als Stilkunstler,* Heidelberg, 1943

English prose, 17C / Browne, Sir Thomas / Personality / Baroque style / Vocabulary

415. 1943 FENIMORE, Edward, "English and Spanish in *For Whom the Bell Tolls,*" *English Literary History,* X (1943), 73–86

◈

Repr., J. K. M. McCaffery, *Ernest Hemingway: The Man and His Work,* Cleveland, 1950, pp. 205–220

American prose, 20C / Hemingway / Spanish idiom / Primitive style

416. 1943 HART, Alfred, "Vocabularies of Shakespeare's Plays," *Review of English Studies,* XIX (1943), 128–140

English drama, 16–17C / Shakespeare / Marlowe / Kyd / Vocabulary count / Hapax legomena / Quantitative methods

417. 1943 HART, Alfred, "The Growth of Shakespeare's Vocabulary," *Review of English Studies,* XIX (1943), 242–254

English drama, 16–17C / Shakespeare / Vocabulary development / Quantitative methods

418. 1943 MACDONALD, Hugh, "Another Aspect of Seventeenth-Century Prose," *Review of English Studies,* XIX (1943), 33–43

Plain style / Reform / Political style / Journalistic style

419. 1943 NEUMANN, J. H., "Jonathan Swift and the Vocabulary of English," *Modern Language Quarterly,* IV (1943), 191–204

English prose, 18C / Swift / Vocabulary / Innovation / Ideals

420. 1943 WALLACE, Karl R., *Francis Bacon on Communication and Rhetoric,* Chapel Hill, N.C., 1943

Rhetoric, Renaissance / Bacon / Oratory

420a 1944 BAX, Clifford, "Style and Fashion in Literature," *Essays by Divers Hands, Being the Transactions of the Royal Society of Literature of the United Kingdom,* N.S., XXI (1944), 67–81

Personality / Value / Multiple styles / Impressionism

421. 1944 FORSTER, E. M., "English Prose Between 1918 and 1939," *Two Cheers for Democracy,* New York, 1951
◈
Repr., *Language, Style, Ideas,* ed. Sumner Ives and Stephen O. Mitchell, New York, 1964, pp. 210–221
English prose, 20C / Innovation / Popularization

*422. 1944 GRAVES, Robert, and Alan HODGE, *The Reader over Your Shoulder,* New York, 1944
◈
Sel., Paul C. Wermuth, *Modern Essays on Writing and Style,* New York, 1964, pp. 155–177
English prose, history / Ars dicendi / Types / Revision

423. 1944 MAJOR, John Campbell, "Matthew Arnold and Attic Prose Style," *PMLA,* LIX (1944), 1086–1103
English prose, 19C / Arnold / Attic style / Ideals

424. 1944 MATTHIESSEN, F. O., "The Painter's Sponge and Varnish Bottle," *Henry James: The Major Phase,* New York, 1963, pp. 152–186
American fiction, 19C / James, Henry / Revision / Chronology

425. 1944 STEUERT, Dom Hilary, "The Place of Allen, Campion and Parsons in the Development of English Prose," *Review of English Studies,* XX (1944), 272–285
English prose, 16C / Allen / Parsons / Campion / Native tradition / Biblical influence / Plain style

426. 1945 BENNETT, H. S., "Fifteenth-Century Secular Prose," *Review of English Studies,* XXI (1945), 257–263
English prose, 15C / Vernacularism

427. 1945 DAVIS, Herbert, "The Conciseness of Swift," *Essays on the Eighteenth Century Presented to David Nichol Smith,* ed. J. R. Sutherland and F. P. Wilson, Oxford, 1945, pp. 15–32

English prose, 18C / Swift / Conciseness / Economy / Plain style / Energy / Internal evidence

428. 1945 DUPEE, F. W., "Difficulty as Style," *The King of the Cats,* New York, 1965, pp. 164–169

English poetry, 20C / Obscurity / Difficult style

429. 1945 NEUMANN, Joshua H., "Milton's Prose Vocabulary," *PMLA,* LX (1945), 102–120

English prose, 17C / Milton / Vocabulary / Innovation / Borrowing / Latinism / Biblical influence / Compounds / Standardization

430. 1945 OLIVER, H. J., "Izaak Walton's Prose Style," *Review of English Studies,* XXI (1945), 280–288

English prose, 17C / Walton / Ornateness / Simplicity / Colloquiality / Euphuism / Faults

431. 1945 RIVANE, Georges, "Le style," *Influence de l'asthme sur l'œuvre de Marcel Proust,* Paris, 1945, pp. 163–173

French prose, 20C / Proust / Sentence structure / Personality / Disease

*432. 1945 SUTHERLAND, James, "Some Aspects of Eighteenth-Century Prose," *Essays on the Eighteenth Century Presented to David Nichol Smith,* ed. J. R. Sutherland and F. P. Wilson, Oxford, 1945, pp. 94–110

English prose, 18C / Plain-ornate / Aristocracy / Conversational style

433. 1945 WILSON, F. P., "Prose," *Elizabethan and Jacobean,* Oxford, 1945, pp. 27–52

English prose, 16–17C / Bacon / Sermon / Ciceronian-Senecan

434. 1946 ANTOINE, Sister M. Salome, *The Rhetoric of Jeremy Taylor's Prose: Ornament of the Sunday Sermons,* Washington, D. C., 1946

English prose, 17C / Taylor / Sermons / Tropes / Figures / Diction / Oratory / Rhetoric, Renaissance / Ciceronian-Senecan

*435. 1946 AUERBACH, Erich, *Mimesis,* tr. Willard Trask, New York, 1957

European literature / Realism / Sociology

435a 1946 BASLER, Roy P., "Lincoln's Development as a Writer," *Abraham Lincoln: His Speeches and Writings,* Cleveland, 1946, pp. 1–49

American prose, 19C / Lincoln / Development / Revision / Rhetoric / Figures

436. 1946 CHRISTENSEN, Francis, "John Wilkins and the Royal Society's Reform of Prose Style," *Modern Language Quarterly,* VII (1946), 179–187, 279–290

English prose, 17C / Wilkins / Royal Society / Reform / Universal language

437. 1946 EKFELDT, Fred Emil, "The Graphic Diction of Milton's English Prose," *Philological Quarterly,* XXV (1946), 46–69

English prose, 17C / Milton / Diction / Concreteness / Colloquiality / Figurative language / Biblical influence / Low style

438. 1946 FLESCH, Rudolf, *The Art of Plain Talk,* New York, 1962

American prose, 20C / Plain style / Sentence length / Ars dicendi

439. 1946 HOWELL, A. C., "*Res et Verba:* Words and Things," *English Literary History,* XIII (1946), 131–142

◈

Sel., Joseph Schwartz and John A. Rycenga, *The Province of Rhetoric,* New York, 1965, pp. 292–308

English prose, 17C / Res et verba / Words-things / Matter-manner / Ideals / Rhetoric, Classical

440. 1946 NEUMANN, J. H., "Chesterfield and the Standard of Usage in English," *Modern Language Quarterly,* VII (1946), 463–475

English prose, 18C / Ideals, 18C / Chesterfield / Correctness / Usage / Aristocracy / Diction / Euphony / Dialect / Slang / French borrowing / Aphorisms

441. 1946 ORWELL, George, "Politics and the English Language," *Selected Essays,* Harmondsworth, 1957, pp. 143–157

◈

Repr., Paul C. Wermuth, *Modern Essays on Writing and Style,* New York, 1964, pp. 98–108

English prose, 18C / Swift / Personality / Seriation

442. 1946 SCOTT-THOMAS, Lois M., "The Vocabulary of Jonathan Swift," *Dalhousie Review,* XXV (1946), 442–447

English prose, 18C / Swift / Vocabulary / Innovation

443. 1946 SHORT, R. W., "The Sentence Structure of Henry James," *American Literature,* XVIII (1946), 71–88

American fiction, 19C / James, Henry / Sentence structure / Word-order / Grammar / Rhetoric

444. 1946 STEUERT, Dom Hilary, "The English Prose Style of Thomas Watson, Bishop of Lincoln, 1557," *Modern Language Review,* XLI (1946), 225–236

English prose, 16C / Watson, Thomas / Sermons / Sentence rhythm / Oral style / Learned style

445. 1947 CRESSOT, Marcel, *Le style et ses techniques,* 5th ed., Paris, 1963

French language, inventory / Expressive resources / Words / Rhetoric / Grammar

*446. 1947 MIRIAM JOSEPH, Sister, *Shakespeare's Use of the Arts of Language,* New York, 1966

◈

Abridged, *Rhetoric in Shakespeare's Time,* New York, 1962

English drama, 16–17C / Shakespeare / Rhetoric, Renaissance / Rhetoric, Classical / Imagery / Figures / Tropes

447. 1947 TUVE, Rosemond, *Elizabethan and Metaphysical Imagery,* Chicago, 1963

◈

Sel., Joseph Schwartz and John A. Rycenga, *The Province of Rhetoric,* New York, 1965, pp. 414–425

English poetry, 16–17C / Poetics / Imagery / Rhetoric, Renaissance

448. 1948 ALLEN, Don Cameron, "Style and Certitude," *English Literary History,* XV (1948), 167–175

English prose, 17C / Senecan style / Reflection theory

449. 1948 EMERY, Clark, "John Wilkins' Universal Language," *Isis,* XXXVIII (1948), 174–185

English language / Wilkins / Universal language / Prose reform

450. 1948 FROHOCK, W. M., "Thomas Wolfe: Of Time and Neurosis," *The Novel of Violence in America 1900–1950,* Dallas, 1950, pp. 47–66

◈

Sel., *Thomas Wolfe,* ed. C. Hugh Holman, New York, 1962, pp. 69–71

American fiction, 20C / Wolfe, Thomas / Rhetorical prose

451. 1948 GODIN, Henri J. G., *Les ressources stylistiques du français contemporain,* Oxford, 1948

French language, inventory / Syntax / Translation / Lexicon

452. 1948 JOHNSON, Pamela Hansford, "The Style," *Hungry Gulliver,* New York, 1948, pp. 20–39

◈

Sel., *Thomas Wolfe,* ed. C. Hugh Holman, New York, 1962, pp. 64–68

American fiction, 20C / Wolfe, Thomas / Poetical prose

453. 1948 MASTERSON, James R., and Wendell Brooks PHILLIPS, *Federal Prose,* Chapel Hill, N.C., 1948

American prose, 20C / Reform / Purism / Jargon

453a 1948–51 MILES, Josephine, *The Continuity of Poetic Language,* New York, 1965

English poetry, 16–20C / Diction / Nouns / Verbs / Adjectives / Keywords

454. 1948 MOUTON, Jean, *Le style de Marcel Proust,* Paris, 1948

French fiction, 20C / Proust / Theory / Formation / Imagery / Rhythm / Enumeration / Dialogue

455. 1948 WIMSATT, W. K., Jr., *Philosophic Words,* New Haven, 1948

English prose, 18C / Johnson / Vocabulary / Heavy diction / Lexicography

456. 1949 DOBREE, Bonamy, "Some Aspects of Defoe's Prose," *Pope and His Contemporaries,* ed. J. L. Clifford and L. A. Landa, Oxford, 1949, pp. 171–184

English prose, 18C / Defoe / Multiple styles

457. 1949 ELDERTON, W. P., "A Few Statistics on the Length of English Words," *Journal of the Royal Statistical Society,* CXII (1949), 436–443

English language / Word-length / Quantitative methods / Statistics

458. 1949 HIGHET, Gilbert, "Baroque Prose," *The Classical Tradition,* New York, 1949, pp. 322–354

English prose, 16–17C / Rhetoric, Classical / Baroque prose / Ciceronian prose

459. 1949 HILLES, Frederick W., "Sir Joshua's Prose," *The Age of Johnson: Essays Presented to C. B. Tinker,* New Haven, 1949, pp. 49–60

English prose, 18C / Reynolds / Johnsonian style / Diction / Rhetoric

459a 1949 MACK, Maynard, " 'Wit and Poetry in Pope': Some Observations on His Imagery," *Pope and His Contemporaries: Essays Presented to George Sherburn,* ed. James L. Clifford and Louis A. Landa, Oxford, 1949, pp. 20–40

English poetry, 18C / Pope / Metaphor / Figures / Prosaism

460. 1949 PARTRIDGE, A. C., *The Problem of Henry VIII Reopened,* Cambridge, 1949

English drama, 16–17C / Shakespeare / Fletcher / Verbs / Vocabulary / Attribution

461. 1950 DE VOTO, Bernard, "The World of Fiction," *The World of Fiction,* Boston, 1950, pp. 260–264

◈
Sel., *Thomas Wolfe,* ed. C. Hugh Holman, New York, 1962, pp. 72–74

American prose, 20C / Wolfe, Thomas / Rhetorical prose / Bad style / Errors

462. 1950 KRISHNAMURTI, S., "Dr. Johnson's Use of Monosyllabic Words," *Journal of the University of Bombay,* XIX (1950), 1–12

English prose, 18C / Johnson / Nouns / Monosyllabism / Attribution / Quantitative methods

463. 1950 WEDGWOOD, C. V., *Seventeenth-Century English Literature,* New York, 1961

English prose, 17C / Typology / Sermon

464. 1951 BRADBROOK, Frank W., "Style and Judgment in Jane Austen's Novels," *Cambridge Journal,* IV (1951), 515–537

English fiction, 19C / Austen / Dialogue / Clichés / Characterization

465. 1951 CLEMEN, Wolfgang, *The Development of Shakespeare's Imagery,* New York, n.d.

English drama, 16–17C / Shakespeare / Imagery / Symbol / Ambiguity / Consistency

466. 1951 CRANE, Milton, *Shakespeare's Prose,* Chicago, 1963

English prose, 16–17C / Shakespeare / Dramatic prose

467. 1951 DAVIE, Donald A., "Berkeley's Style in *Siris*," *Cambridge Journal*, IV (1951), 427–433

English prose, 18C / Berkeley / Metaphor / Diction

468. 1951 DAVIS, Herbert, "The Conversation of the Augustans," *The Seventeenth Century*, Stanford, 1951, pp. 181–197

English language, 18C / Swift / Conversation / Aristocratic influence

468a 1951 HILL, Archibald A., "Correctness and Style in English Composition," *College English*, XII (1951), 280–285

English language / Correctness / Errors / Teaching

469. 1951 KRISHNAMURTI, S., "Frequency Distribution of Nouns in Dr. Johnson's Prose Works," *Journal of the University of Bombay*, XX (1951), 1–16

English prose, 18C / Johnson / Nouns / Attribution / Quantitative methods

*470. 1951 LANNERING, Jan, *Studies in the Prose Style of Joseph Addison*, Upsala, 1951

English prose, 18C / Addison / Ideals / Diction / Seriation

*471. 1951 LEVIN, Harry, "Observations on the Style of Hemingway," *Kenyon Review*, XIII (1951), 581–609 ◈

Repr., *Hemingway*, ed. Robert P. Weeks, Englewood Cliffs, N.J., 1962, pp. 72–85

American fiction, 20C / Hemingway / Poetic style / Seriation / Connection / Diction / Verbal skepticism

472. 1951 MILES, Josephine, "The Language of the Donne Tradition," *Kenyon Review*, XIII (1951), 37–49

English poetry, 17C / Donne / Metrics / Sound / Diction / Grammar / Parts of speech / Imagery

473. 1951 MORGAN, Edwin, "'Strong Lines' and Strong Minds," *Cambridge Journal,* IV (1951), 481–491

English poetry, 17C / Strong lines / Conceits

474. 1951 STEIN, Arnold, "Structures of Sound in Donne's Verse," *Kenyon Review,* XIII (1951), 20–36, 256–278

English poetry, 17C / Donne / Metrics / Poetics / Sound / Metaphor

475. 1951 SUMMERSGILL, Travis L., "The Influence of the Marprelate Controversy upon the Style of Thomas Nashe," *Studies in Philology,* XLVIII (1951), 145–160

English prose, 16C / Nashe / Euphuism / Puritan style / Alteration

476. 1951 WARREN, Austin, "The Style of Browne," *Kenyon Review,* XIII (1951), 674–687

English prose, 17C / Browne / Expressive theory / Prose rhythm / Diction / Sentence structure / Multiple styles / Meaning

*477. 1951 WILLIAMSON, George, *The Senecan Amble,* London, 1951

English prose, 17C / Ciceronian-Senecan / Rhetoric, Renaissance / Plain style

478. 1952 DAVIE, Donald, "Irony and Conciseness in Berkeley and Swift," *Dublin Magazine,* N. S. XXVII (1952), 20–29

English prose, 18C / Berkeley / Swift / Irony / Conciseness

479. 1952 EVANS, B. Ifor, *The Language of Shakespeare's Plays,* London, 1965

English drama, 16–17C / Shakespeare / Impressionism

480. 1952 FISCH, H., "The Puritans and the Reform of Prose Style," *English Literary History,* XIX (1952), 229–248

English prose, 17C / Sermon / Reform / Plain style / Imagery / Matter-manner

481. 1952 FREIMARCK, Vincent, "The Bible and Neo-Classical Views of Style," *Journal of English and Germanic Philology,* LI (1952), 507–526

English prose, 18C / Bible / Ideals, 18C / Diction / Metaphor / Decorum

482. 1952 KRISHNAMURTI, S., "Vocabulary Tests Applied to (Dr. Johnson's) Authorship of the 'Misargyrus' Papers in the Adventurer," *Journal of the University of Bombay,* XXI (1952), 47–62

English prose, 18C / Johnson / Attribution / Internal evidence / Vocabulary / Yule / Quantitative methods

483. 1952 WHYTE, William H., Jr., "The Language of Business," "The Prose Engineers," *Is Anybody Listening?,* New York, 1952, pp. 46–64, 65–80

English prose, 20C / Jargon / Readability / Plain style

484. 1952 YOUNG, Philip, "The Origins and Meaning of a Style," *Ernest Hemingway,* New York, 1952, pp. 144–180

American fiction, 20C / Hemingway / Formation / Influence / Sources / Development / Impressionism

*485. 1953 BARTHES, Roland, *Le degré zéro de l'écriture,* Paris, 1953

French prose, 20C / Camus / Neutral style / Deterioration

486. 1953 CHASE, Stuart, "Gobbledygook," *Power of Words,* New York, 1953

◈

Repr., *Exposition and the English Language,* ed. James L. Sanderson and Walter K. Gordon, New York, 1963, pp. 411–419

American prose, 20C / Purism / Jargon / Reform / Nominal style

487. 1953 DOUGLAS, Wallace W., "Souls Among Masterpieces: The Solemn Style of Modern Critics," *American Scholar,* XXIII (1953), 43–55

English prose, 20C / Critical writing

488. 1953 HENDRICK, Leo Thomas, "Henry James: The Late and Early Styles (A Stylistics Study)," *Dissertation Abstracts,* XIII (1953), 808–809

American fiction, 19C / James, Henry / Chronology / Personality / Syntax / Sentence-length

489. 1953 KRISHNAMURTI, S., "Vocabulary Tests Applied to the Authorship of the 'New Essays' Attributed to Dr. Johnson," *Journal of the University of Bombay,* XXII (1953), 1–5

English prose, 18C / Johnson / Attribution / Vocabulary / Quantitative methods

490. 1953 JONES, Richard Foster, *The Triumph of the English Language,* Stanford, 1953

English prose, history / Vocabulary / Reform / Borrowing

491. 1953 PRICE, Martin, *Swift's Rhetorical Art,* New Haven, 1953

English prose, 18C / Swift / Rhetoric / Irony / Persona / Multiple styles

492. 1953 SEIDLER, Herbert, *Allgemeine Stilistik,* Göttingen, 1953

German language, inventory / Theory

493. 1953 WHYTE, William H., Jr., "You, Too, Can Write the Casual Style," *Harper's,* CCVII (Oct. 1953), 87–89

American prose, 20C / Casual style / Diction / Syntax

494. 1954 BLANSHARD, Brand, *On Philosophical Style,* Manchester, 1954

English prose, 19C / Philosophical style / Ars dicendi / Ideals

495. 1954 BOULTON, Marjorie, *The Anatomy of Prose,* London, 1962

English prose / Rhetoric / Ars dicendi / Elements / Typology

496. 1954 BRADBROOK, M. C., "Fifty Years of the Criticism of Shakespeare's Style: A Retrospect," *Shakespeare Survey* 7, ed. Allardyce Nicoll, Cambridge, 1954, pp. 1–11

English drama, 16–17C / Shakespeare / Survey / Grammar / Vocabulary / Spelling / Pronunciation / Prosody / Rhetoric / Imagery

497. 1954 COHEN, Marcel, *Grammaire et style, 1450–1950,* Paris, 1954

French language / Sociology / Levels / Stylistic resources

498. 1954 EWALD, William B., *The Masks of Jonathan Swift,* Oxford, 1954

English prose, 18C / Swift / Rhetorical devices / Persona

499. 1954 HIGHET, Gilbert, "The Gettysburg Address," *A Clerk of Oxenford,* New York, 1954

◈

Repr., *Readings in Speech,* ed. Haig A. Bosmajian, New York, 1965, pp. 240–246

American prose, 19C / Lincoln / Rhetorical devices / Speech / Allusion / Imagery

499a 1954 O'BRIEN, Justin, "Proust's Use of Syllepsis," *PMLA,* LXIX (1954), 741–752

French fiction, 20C / Proust / Figures / Sentences / Zeugma

500. 1954 WILLCOCK, Gladys D., "Shakespeare and Elizabethan English," *Shakespeare Survey 7,* ed. Allardyce Nicoll, Cambridge, 1954, pp. 12–24

English language, 16C / Shakespeare / Rhetoric, Renaissance / Diction / Colloquiality / Grammar / Innovation

501. 1955 DAVIE, Donald, *Articulate Energy,* London, 1955

English poetry / Syntax / Aesthetics / Grammar / Poetics

502. 1955 DOBREE, Bonamy, "Some Remarks on Prose in England Today," *Sewanee Review,* LXIII (1955), 631–646

English prose, 20C / Personality / Plain prose / Flat style / Impersonal style / Prose-poetry / Stereotypes / Vivid writing

503. 1955 MOORE, Geoffrey, "American Prose Today," *New World Writing No. 8,* New York, 1955, pp. 47–70

◈

Repr., *Essays on Language and Usage,* ed. Leonard F. Dean and Kenneth G. Wilson, 2d ed., New York, 1963, pp. 337–354

American prose, 20C / Types / Levels

504. 1955 SCHUSTER, Sister Mary Faith, "Philosophy of Life and Prose Style in Thomas More's *Richard III* and Francis Bacon's *Henry VII*," *PMLA*, LXX (1955), 474–487

English prose, 16C / More / Bacon / Sentence / Ciceronianism / Reflection theory

505. 1955 THURBER, James, "The Psychosemanticist Will See You Now, Mr. Thurber," *New Yorker*, XXXI (May 28, 1955), 28–31

American prose, 20C / Reform / Diction / Jargon

506. 1956 BARISH, Jonas A., "The Prose Style of John Lyly," *English Literary History*, XXIII (1956), 14–35

English prose, 16C / Lyly / Euphuism / Antithesis / Paradox

507. 1956 COWLEY, Malcolm, "Sociological Habit Patterns in Linguistic Transmogrification," *Reporter*, XV (Sept. 20, 1956), 41–43

American prose, 20C / Sociological prose / Jargon / Nominal style / Purism / Vocabulary / Syntax

508. 1956 EHRENPREIS, Irvin, "Introduction," *Jonathan Swift: An Enquiry into the Behavior of the Queen's Last Ministry*, ed. Irvin Ehrenpreis, Bloomington, Ind., 1956, pp. xi–xliii

English prose, 18C / Swift / Revision / Alteration / Unconsciousness

*509. 1956 HERDAN, Gustav, "Chaucer's Authorship of *The Equatorie of the Planetis*," *Language*, XXXII (1956), 254–259

English language, 14C / Chaucer / Attribution / Internal evidence / Quantitative methods / Vocabulary / Rank-order / Native-Romance ratio

510. 1956 KING, J. R., "Certain Aspects of Jeremy Taylor's Prose Style," *English Studies,* XXXVII (1956), 197–210

English prose, 17C / Taylor / Ciceronian style / Prose rhythm

*511. 1956 SUTHERLAND, James R., "Restoration Prose," *Restoration and Augustan Prose,* Los Angeles, 1956, pp. 1–18

English prose, 17C / Restoration prose / Conversation / Aristocracy

512. 1956 THOMSON, J. A. K., *Classical Influences on English Prose,* London, 1956

English prose / Classical influence / Rhetoric, Classical / Types

513. 1956 WATT, Ian, "The Ironic Tradition in Augustan Prose from Swift to Johnson," *Restoration and Augustan Prose,* Los Angeles, 1956, pp. 19–46

English prose, 18C / Swift / Johnson / Augustan prose / Irony

514. 1957 LEVIN, Harry, "The War of Words in English Poetry," *Contexts of Criticism,* New York, 1963, pp. 208–233

English poetry / Poetics / Levels / Vocabulary

515. 1957 MORTON, A. Q., "The Structure of the New Testament," *Science News 43,* Harmondsworth, 1957, pp. 19–30

Bible / Line length / Textual editing / Quantitative methods

516. 1957 NATANSON, Maurice, "The Privileged Moment: A Study in the Rhetoric of Thomas Wolfe," *Quarterly Journal of Speech,* XLIII (1957), 143–150

◈

(Continued)

Repr., *Thomas Wolfe,* ed. C. Hugh Holman, New York, 1962, pp. 78–84

American fiction, 20C / Wolfe / Rhetorical style / Personality

517. 1957 RIFFATERRE, Michael, *Le style des Pléiades de Gobineau,* Geneva, 1957

French poetry, 19C / Gobineau / Expressivity / Stylistic function / Diction / Seriation / Repetition / Concreteness / Imagery

518. 1957 ROELLINGER, Francis X., Jr., "The Early Development of Carlyle's Style," *PMLA,* LXXII (1957), 936–951

English prose, 19C / Carlyle / Formation / Multiple styles / Personality

519. 1957 STRAUSS, Walter A., "Conclusion," *Proust and Literature,* Cambridge, Mass., 1957, pp. 209–227

◈

Repr. "Criticism and Creation," *Proust,* ed. René Girard, Englewood Cliffs, N.J., 1962, pp. 53–68

French fiction, 20C / Proust / Theory / Definition

*520. 1957 SUTHERLAND, James R., *On English Prose,* Toronto, 1957

English prose, 17–18C / New style / Aristocracy / Conversation / Colloquiality

*521. 1957 ULLMANN, Stephen, *Style in the French Novel,* Oxford, 1964

French fiction, 19–20C / Proust / Flaubert / Goncourts / Survey / Linguistics / Semantics / Reported discourse / Word-order / Imagery

522. 1957 WATKINS, Floyd C., "Rhetoric in Southern Writing: Wolfe," *Georgia Review,* XII (1958), 79–82
◈
Repr., *Thomas Wolfe,* ed. C. Hugh Holman, New York, 1962, pp. 75–77
American fiction, 20C / Wolfe / Rhetorical style

523. 1958 AUERBACH, Erich, *Literary Language and Its Public in Late Latin Antiquity and in the Middle Ages,* tr. Ralph Manheim, New York, 1965
Latin language / Rhetoric, medieval / Vernacular

524. 1958 BERRY, Francis, *Poets' Grammar,* London, 1958
English poetry / Grammar / Parts of speech

*525. 1958 BROOKE-ROSE, Christine, *A Grammar of Metaphor,* London, 1965
English poetry / Parts of speech / Grammar / Imagery

526. 1958 CHANDLER, Edmund, *Pater on Style,* Copenhagen, 1958
Pater / Theory / Ideals, 19C / Revision / Vocabulary / Sentence

527. 1958 GRAY, Floyd, *Le style de Montaigne,* Paris, 1958
French prose, 16C / Montaigne / Grammar / Syntax / Vocabulary / Imagery

528. 1958 GREENBURG, Dan, "Three Bears in Search of an Author: Catch Her in the Oatmeal," *Esquire,* XLIX (Feb. 1958), 46–67
◈

(Continued)

Repr., *Language, Style, Ideas,* ed. Sumner Ives and Stephen O. Mitchell, New York, 1964, pp. 206–207

American fiction, 20C / Salinger / Parody

529. 1958 LORD, George de F., "Two New Poems by Marvell?" *Bulletin of the New York Public Library,* LXII (1958), 551–570

English poetry, 17C / Marvell / Attribution / Eclectic method

530. 1958 STEVENSON, Lionel, "Meredith and the Problem of Style in the Novel," *Zeitschrift für Anglistik und Amerikanistik,* VI (1958), 181–189 ◈

Repr., *Stil- und Formprobleme in der Literatur,* ed. Paul Böckmann, Heidelberg, 1959, pp. 339–343

English fiction, 19C / Meredith / Vernacularity / Obscurity / Poetic prose / Conversation

531. 1959 ALLEN, Gay W., "The Problem of Metaphor in Translating Walt Whitman's *Leaves of Grass,*" *English Studies Today, Second Series,* ed. G. A. Bonnard, Berne, 1961, pp. 269–280

American poetry, 19C / Whitman / Imagery / Diction / Connotation / Incoherence / French language / Translation

532. 1959 BARZUN, Jacques, "Lincoln: The Literary Genius," *Saturday Evening Post* (Feb. 14, 1959), pp. 30, 62–64

American prose, 19C / Lincoln / Plain style / Formation

533. 1959 BLACKALL, Eric A., "The Language of Sturm und Drang," *Stil- und Formprobleme in der Literatur,* ed. Paul Böckmann, Heidelberg, 1959, pp. 272–283

German language, 18C / Goethe / Klopstock /Sturm und Drang style / Rhetorical style

534. 1959 BROWER, Reuben A., "Seven Agamemnons," *On Translation,* ed. Reuben A. Brower, Cambridge, Mass., 1959, pp. 173–195

Translation, Classical / Aeschylus / Definition

535. 1959 COSTELLO, Donald P., "The Language of *The Catcher in the Rye,*" *American Speech,* XXXIV (1959), 172–181

◈

Repr., *Aspects of American English,* ed. Elizabeth M. Kerr and Ralph M. Aderman, New York, 1963, pp. 167–176

American fiction, 20C / Salinger / Diction / Syntax / Characterization

536. 1959 CROW, Charles R., "The Style of Henry James: *The Wings of the Dove,*" *Style in Prose Fiction,* ed. Harold C. Martin, New York, 1959, pp. 172–189

American fiction, 19C / James, Henry / Chronology / Impressionism

537. 1959 DOUGLAS, Wallace, "Introduction," *The Character of Prose,* Boston, 1959, pp. 1023–1038

English prose, 20C / Modern style

538. 1959 FANG, Achilles, "Some Reflections on the Difficulty of Translation," *On Translation,* ed. Reuben A. Brower, Cambridge, Mass., 1959, pp. 111–133

Chinese language / Translation

539. 1959 FITTS, Dudley, "The Poetic Nuance," *On*

Translation, ed. Reuben A. Brower, Cambridge, Mass., 1959, pp. 32–47

Poetry / Translation / Poeticalness

540. 1959 FUSSELL, Paul, Jr., "Speaker and Style in *A Letter of Advice to a Young Poet* (1721), and the Problem of Attribution," *Review of English Studies,* X (1959), 63–67

English prose, 18C / Swift / Attribution / Persona / Multiple styles

541. 1959 GERBER, John C., "The Relation between Point of View and Style in the Works of Mark Twain," *Style in Prose Fiction,* ed. Harold C. Martin, New York, 1959, pp. 142–171

American prose, 19C / Twain / Multiple styles / Point of view / Evaluation

542. 1959 HUMPHRIES, Rolfe, "Latin and English Verse—Some Practical Considerations," *On Translation,* ed. Reuben A. Brower, Cambridge, Mass., 1959, pp. 57–66

Translation / Poetry / Diction / Prosody / Latin language

543. 1959 JOHNSON, S. F., "Hardy and Burke's *Sublime,*" *Style in Prose Fiction,* ed. Harold C. Martin, New York, 1959, pp. 55–86

English prose, 18–19C / Hardy / Burke / Formation

544. 1959 KNIGHT, Douglas, "Translation: The Augustan Mode," *On Translation,* ed. Reuben A. Brower, Cambridge, Mass., 1959, pp. 196–204

English poetry, 18C / Pope / Translation

545. 1959 LATTIMORE, Richmond, "Practical Notes on Translating Greek Poetry," *On Translation,* ed.

Reuben A. Brower, Cambridge, Mass., 1959, pp. 48–56

Translation / Greek poetry / Diction

546. 1959 MARTIN, Harold C., "The Development of Style in Nineteenth-Century American Fiction," *Style in Prose Fiction,* ed. Harold C. Martin, New York, 1959, pp. 114–141

American prose, 19C / Native style / Diction / Syntax

547. 1959 MATHEWS, Jackson, "Third Thoughts on Translating Poetry," *On Translation,* ed. Reuben A. Brower, Cambridge, Mass., 1959, pp. 67–77

Poetry / Translation / Prose-verse

548. 1959 MORTIER, Roland, "Le style du Cardinal de Retz," *Stil- und Formprobleme in der Literatur,* ed. Paul Böckmann, Heidelberg, 1959, pp. 201–208

French prose, 17C / Retz / Impressionism

549. 1959 MUIR, Edwin and Willa, "Translating from the German," *On Translation,* ed. Reuben A. Brower, Cambridge, Mass., 1959, pp. 93–96

Translation / German language / National character / Multiple styles

550. 1959 NABOKOV, Vladimir, "The Servile Path," *On Translation,* ed. Reuben A. Brower, Cambridge, Mass., 1959, pp. 97–110

Translation / Russian language / Borrowing / Pushkin

551. 1959 O'BRIEN, Justin, "From French to English," *On Translation,* ed. Reuben A. Brower, Cambridge, Mass., 1959, pp. 97–110

Translation / Vocabulary / French language

552. 1959 PRESCOTT, Joseph, "Stylistic Realism in Joyce's *Ulysses,*" *Stil- und Formprobleme in der Literatur,* ed. Paul Böckmann, Heidelberg, 1959, pp. 427–429

English fiction, 20C / Joyce / Revision / Vocabulary / Innovation

552a 1959 QUIRK, Randolph, *Charles Dickens and Appropriate Language,* Durham, 1959

English fiction, 19C / Dickens / Linguistic views / Linguistic knowledge / Phonetics / Graphemics

553. 1959 READ, Herbert, "The Style of Criticism," *English Studies Today, Second Series,* ed G. A. Bonnard, Berne, 1961, pp. 29–41

English criticism, 20C / Critical writing / Idiosyncratic style / Value / Aesthetics

554. 1959 STEDMOND, J. M., "Style and *Tristram Shandy,*" *Modern Language Quarterly,* XX (1959), 243–251

English fiction, 18C / Sterne / Conversational style / Influence / Senecan style

555. 1959 STRAUSS, Albrecht B., "On Smollett's Language: A Paragraph in *Ferdinand Count Fathom,*" *Style in Prose Fiction,* ed. Harold C. Martin, New York, 1959, pp. 25–54

English fiction, 18C / Smollett / Evaluation / Diction / Stereotypes

556. 1959 TILLYARD, E. M. W., "The Literary Kinds and Milton," *Stil- und Formprobleme in der Literatur,* ed. Paul Böckmann, Heidelberg, 1959, pp. 95–103

Milton / Thackeray / Genre / Types

557. 1959 WILKINSON, Elizabeth, "'Form' and 'Content' in the Aesthetics of German Classicism," *Stil- und Formprobleme in der Literatur,* ed. Paul Böckmann, Heidelberg, 1959, pp. 18–27

German literature, 18C / Aesthetics / Form-content

558. 1959 ZOELLNER, Robert H., "Faulkner's Prose Style in *Absalom, Absalom!*" *American Literature,* XXX (1959), 486–502

American fiction, 20C / Faulkner / Sentence structure / Complication / Structural ambiguity / Dependence / Suspension / Reflection theory

558a 1960 BACH, Emmon, "The Syntax of Hölderlin's Poems: I," *Texas Studies in Literature and Language,* II (1960), 383–397
(*See also* No. 577a)

German poetry, 18C / Hölderlin / Syntax / Sentence length / Verbs / Quantitative methods / Statistics

559. 1960 BARISH, Jonas A., *Ben Jonson and the Language of Prose Comedy,* Cambridge, Mass., 1960

English prose, 17C / Jonson / Rhetoric, Elizabethan / Euphuism

560. 1960 BOND, H. L., "Language," *The Literary Art of Edward Gibon,* Oxford, 1960, pp. 136–158

English prose, 18C / Gibbon / Word order / Prose rhythm / Sentence structure / Diction / Rhetoric

561. 1960 BROWN, Roger, and Albert GILMAN, "The Pronouns of Power and Solidarity," *Style in Language,* ed. Thomas A. Sebeok, Cambridge, Mass. and New York, pp. 253–276

Pronouns / Indo-European languages / Sociology

562. 1960 CHARLESTON, Britta M., *Studies on the Emotional and Affective Means of Expression in Modern English,* Berne, 1960

English language, inventory / Affectivity / Stylistic devices / Expressive theory

563. 1960 DAVIE, Donald, "Syntax and Music in 'Paradise Lost,'" *The Living Milton,* ed. F. Kermode, New York, 1961, pp. 70–84

English poetry, 17C / Milton / Syntax / Musical verse

564. 1960 DAVIES, Hugh Sykes, "Trollope and His Style," *Review of English Literature,* I (1960), 73–85

English fiction, 19C / Trollope / Sentence structure / Cadence / Connectives

565. 1960 DORSON, Richard M., "Oral Styles of American Folk Narrators," *Style in Language,* ed. Thomas A. Sebeok, Cambridge, Mass. and New York, pp. 27–53

Folk narration / Oral style / American speech

566. 1960 FRASER, G. S., "Macaulay's Style as an Essayist," *Review of English Literature,* I (1960), 9–19

English prose, 19C / Macaulay / Victorian style / Antithesis / Rhetoric / Personality

567. 1960 GANDON, Yves, *Le démon du style,* rev. ed., Paris, 1960

French prose, 20C / Value / Ars dicendi / Types

568. 1960 GRAHAM, John, "Ernest Hemingway: The Meaning of Style," *Modern Fiction Studies,* VI (1960), 298–313

◈

Repr., *Ernest Hemingway,* ed. Carlos Baker, New York, 1962, pp. 183–192

American fiction, 20C / Hemingway / Perception / Point of view

569. 1960 LEED, Jacob, "Two Notes on Johnson and *The Gentleman's Magazine,*" *Papers of the Bibliographical Society of America,* LIV (1960), 101–110

English prose, 18C / Johnson / Attribution / Internal evidence / Diction

*570. 1960 MILES, Josephine, *Renaissance, Eighteenth-Century, and Modern Language in English Poetry,* Berkeley and Los Angeles, 1960

English poetry / English language / Parts of speech / Quantitative methods

571. 1960 MOSER, Edwin, "A Critical Examination of the Canon of the Prose Writings of Samuel Johnson," *Dissertation Abstracts,* XX (1960), 3283–3284

English prose, 18C / Johnson / Impressionism / Attribution / Internal evidence / Prose rhythm / Rhetorical devices

572. 1960 RIDENOUR, George M., *The Style of Don Juan,* New Haven, 1960

English poetry, 19C / Byron / Rhetoric, Classical / Metaphor

573. 1960 ROCKAS, Leo, "The Description of Style: Dr. Johnson and His Critics," *Dissertation Abstracts,* XXI (1961), 338–339

English prose, 18C / Johnson / Descriptive methods

574. 1960 SLATOFF, Walter J., "Stylistic Antithesis," *Quest for Failure: A Study of William Faulkner,* Ithaca, N.Y., 1960, pp. 122–127

American fiction, 20C / Faulkner / Antithesis / Polarity / Syntax / Negativity

*575. 1960 ULLMANN, Stephen, *The Image in the Modern French Novel,* Oxford, 1963

French fiction, 20C / Gide / Alain-Fournier / Proust / Camus / Imagery / Metaphor / Symbolism / Neutral style

575a 1960 WATT, Ian, "The First Paragraph of *The Ambassadors:* An Explication," *Essays in Criticism,* X (1960), 250–274
◈
Repr., Henry James, *The Ambassadors,* ed. S. P. Rosenbaum (Norton Critical Edition), New York, 1964, pp. 465–484

American fiction, 19C / James, Henry / Explication / Syntax / Sentence structure / Eclectic method / Methods

576. 1960 WILSON, F. P., *Seventeenth Century Prose,* Berkeley, 1960

English prose, 17C / Burton / Browne / Sermon

577. 1961 ANDERSON, Charles R., "Hemingway's Other Style," *Modern Language Notes,* LXXVI (1961), 434–442
◈
Repr., *Ernest Hemingway,* ed. Carlos Baker, New York, 1962, pp. 41–46

American fiction, 20C / Hemingway / Multiple styles / Allusion / Imagery

577a 1961 BACH, Emmon, "The Syntax of Hölderlin's Poems: II," *Texas Studies in Literature and Language,* II (1961), 444–457
(*See also* No. 558a)

German poetry, 18C / Hölderlin / Syntax / Syntactic types

578. 1961 BEAUMONT, Charles Allen, *Swift's Classical Rhetoric,* Athens, Ga., 1961

◈

Sel., Joseph Schwartz and John A. Rycenga, *The Province of Rhetoric,* New York, 1965, pp. 455–481

English prose, 18C / Swift / Rhetoric, Classical / Oration / Figures

579. 1961 BLACKALL, Eric A., "The Imprint of Herder's Linguistic Theory on his Early Prose Style," *PMLA,* LXXVI (1961), 512–518

German prose, 18C / Herder / Linguistic theory / Formation / Theory

580. 1961 DAVIS, Norman, "Styles in English Prose of the Late Middle and Early Modern Period," *Langue et littérature* (Proceedings of the Eighth Congress, International Federation for Modern Languages and Literatures, Liège, 1960), Paris, 1961, pp. 165–181

English prose, 14–16C / Types / Rhythm / Speech

581. 1961 GEORGIN, René, *Les secrets du style,* Paris, 1961

French language / Ars dicendi / Grammar / Rhetoric

582. 1961 KENNEY, William, "Addison, Johnson, and the 'Energetick' Style," *Studia Neophilologica,* XXXIII (1961), 103–114

English prose, 18C / Addison / Johnson / Energetic style / Ideals, 18C

583. 1961 MILES, Josephine, "The Primary Language of *Lycidas*," *Milton's Lycidas,* ed. C. A. Patrides, New York, 1961, pp. 95–100

English poetry, 17C / Milton / Parts of speech / Diction / Repetition

584. 1961 NORMAN, Charles, "Winston Churchill: Author," *Bulletin of the New York Public Library,* LXV (1961), 154–158

English prose, 20C / Churchill / Formation / Reading / Influence

585. 1961 QUIRK, Randolph, "Some Observations on the Language of Dickens," *Review of English Literature,* II (1961), 19–28

English fiction, 19C / Dickens / Slang / Vocabulary / Syntax

586. 1961 SWIECZKOWSKI, Walerian, "On the Margin of Syntax and Style (A Quantitative Study)," *Poetics,* Warsaw, 1961, pp. 463–469

Pronominal substitution / Reference / Connection / Sentences / Quantitative methods

587. 1962 BARBER, C. L., "Some Measurable Characteristics of Modern Scientific Prose," *Contributions to English Syntax and Philology,* Göteborg, 1962, pp. 21–43

English prose, 20C / Scientific prose / Syntax / Quantitative methods

588. 1962 BRADY, Frank, "Prose Style and the 'Whig' Tradition," *Bulletin of the New York Public Library,* LXVI (1962), 455–463

English prose, 18C / Burke / Whig prose / Political style

589. 1962 ELLEGÅRD, Alvar, *Who Was Junius?*, Stockholm, 1962

English prose, 18C / Junius / Attribution / Internal evidence / Vocabulary / Quantitative methods / Statistics / Computers

590. 1962 GALINSKY, Hans, "The Expatriate Poet's Style," *English Studies Today, Third Series*, ed. G. I. Duthie, Edinburgh, 1964, pp. 215–226

English poetry, 20C / Eliot / Auden / Americanism

591. 1962 GREENE, Donald J., "Is there a 'Tory' Prose Style?" *Bulletin of the New York Public Library*, LXVI (1962), 449–454

English prose, 18C / Tory prose / Political style / Figurative language

591a 1962 HNATKO, Eugene, "Studies in the Prose Style of Laurence Sterne," *Dissertation Abstracts*, XXIII (1963), 4685

English prose, 18C / Sterne / Eclectic methods / Syntax / Impressionism

592. 1962 HODGART, Matthew, "Politics and Prose Style in the Late Eighteenth Century: The Radicals," *Bulletin of the New York Public Library*, LXVI (1962), pp. 464–469

English prose, 18C / Paine / Godwin / Radical prose / Political style

593. 1962 HULME, Hilda M., *Explorations in Shakespeare's Language*, London, 1962

English drama, 16–17C / Shakespeare / Vocabulary / Meaning / Proverbs / Latinism / Spelling / Context

594. 1962 JOOS, Martin, "Homeostasis in English Usage," *College Composition and Communication,* XIII (1962), 18–22

English prose, 20C / Levels / Types / Usage

595. 1962 LAWTON, George, *John Wesley's English: A Study of His Literary Style,* London, 1962

English prose, 18C / Wesley / Vocabulary / Imagery / Sermon

595a 1962 LEGROS, Georges, "Sartre a-t-il un style?" *Cahiers d'analyse textuelle,* IV (1962), 97–109

French fiction, 20C / Sartre / Value / Explication

596. 1962 MAROUZEAU, J., *Traité de stylistique latine,* 4th ed., Paris, 1962

Latin language / Resources / Grammar

*597. 1962 OHMANN, Richard M., *Shaw: The Style and the Man,* Middletown, Conn., 1962

English prose, 19–20C / Shaw / Seriation / Comparison / Negation / Syntax / Semantics / Conceptualization

598. 1962 ROGER, Jacques, "Introduction—l'écrivain," *Buffon: les époques de la nature* (Mémoires du muséum national d'histoire naturelle, nouvelle série, Tome X), Paris, 1962, pp. cxiv–cxxvii

French prose, 18C / Buffon / Scientific prose / Rhetoric / Prose rhythm

599. 1962 SHERBO, Arthur, "Samuel Johnson and *The Gentleman's Magazine,* 1750–1755," *Johnsonian Studies,* ed. Magdi Wahba, Cairo, 1962, pp. 133–159

English prose, 18C / Johnson / Attribution / Internal evidence / Vocabulary

600. 1962 TRIMPI, Wesley, *Ben Jonson's Poems: A Study of the Plain Style,* Stanford, Calif., 1962

English poetry, 17C / Jonson / Theory / Ideals, 16–17C / Plain style / Imitation / Levels

601. 1962 TRIMPI, Wesley, "Jonson and the Neo-Latin Authorities for the Plain Style," *PMLA,* LXXII (1962), 21–26

English prose, 17C / Jonson / Plain style / Epistolary style

601a 1962 UITTI, Karl D., "Problems of Style in Language," *Romance Philology,* XV (1962), 424–438 (Rev. of No. 702)

602. 1962 WACKWITZ, Beate, *Die Theorie des Prosastils im England des 18. Jahrhunderts,* Hamburg, 1962

English prose, 18C / Johnson / Theory / Ideals, 18C / Rhetoric

602a 1963 BAR, Francis, "Balzac styliste," *Cahiers de l'association internationale des études françaises,* XV (1963), 308–329

French fiction, 19C / Balzac / Characterization / Imagery / Figures

603. 1963 BROWN, Milton Perry, *The Authentic Writings of Ignatius,* Durham, N.C., 1963

Ignatius / Attribution / Internal evidence / Vocabulary / Grammar

604. 1963 CHRISTENSEN, Francis, "A Lesson from Hemingway," *College English,* XXV (1963), 12–18

American fiction, 20C / Hemingway / Connectives / Sentence structure

605. 1963 DAVIE, Donald, *The Language of Science and the Language of Literature, 1700–1740,* London, 1963
English prose, 18C / Types / Scientific prose / Literary prose

606. 1963 GEORGIN, René, *L'inflation du style,* Paris, 1963
French language / Purism / Pleonasm / Neologism / Anglomania / Clichés / Nominal style

607. 1963 GREENE, Donald J., "The Development of the Johnson Canon," *Restoration and Eighteenth-Century Literature,* ed. Carroll Camden, Chicago, 1963, pp. 407–427
English prose, 18C / Johnson / Canon / Attribution / Internal evidence

608. 1963 JARRELL, Mackie L., "A New Swift Attribution: The Preface to Sheridan's Sermon on St. Cecilia's Day," *PMLA,* LXXVIII (1963), 511–515
English prose, 18C / Swift / Attribution / Internal evidence / Vocabulary / Characteristic terms

609. 1963 MARECHAL, Robert, "La phrase de Marcel Proust," *Le français moderne,* XXXI (1963), 13–30
French fiction, 20C / Proust / Sentence structure / Duration / Connectives

610. 1963 MATTHEWS, William, "Introduction," *Later Medieval English Prose,* New York, 1963, pp. 1–27
English prose, medieval / Typology

611. 1963 MCINTOSH, Angus, "*As You Like It:* A Grammatical Clue to Character," *Review of English Literature,* IV (1963), 68–81
◈

(*Continued*)

Repr., Angus McIntosh and M. A. K. Halliday, *Patterns of Language,* London, 1966, pp. 70–82

English drama, 16–17C / Shakespeare / Characterization / Pronouns

612. 1963 PEARCE, Donald R., "The Style of Milton's Epic," *Yale Review,* LII (1963), 427–444

◈

Repr., *Milton: Modern Essays in Criticism,* ed. Arthur E. Barker, New York, 1965, pp. 368–385

English poetry, 17C / Milton / Artificial style / Rhetoric / Diction / Prosaic style / Formation

613. 1963 RICKS, Christopher, *Milton's Grand Style,* Oxford, 1963

English poetry, 17C / Milton / Grand style / Metaphor / Syntax / Rhythm

614. 1963 ROVIT, Earl, "Of Time and Style," *Ernest Hemingway,* New York, 1963, pp. 126–146

American fiction, 20C / Hemingway / Imagery / Duration

*615 1963 WEBBER, Joan, *Contrary Music: The Prose Style of John Donne,* Madison, Wis., 1963

English prose, 17C / Donne / Rhetoric, Renaissance / Senecan style / Sermon

616. 1964 DEARING, Vinton A., "The Use of a Computer in Analyzing Dryden's Spelling," *Literary Data Processing Conference Proceedings,* ed. Jess B. Bessinger, Stephen M. Parrish and Harry F. Arader, White Plains, N.Y., 1964, pp. 200–210

English language, 17C / Dryden / Spelling / Quantitative methods / Computers

616a 1964 DELHEZ-SARLET, Claudette, "Style indirect libre et 'point de vue' dans *La Princesse de Clèves,*" *Cahiers d'analyse textuelle,* VI (1964), 70–80

French novel, 17C / La Fayette / Point of view / Indirect style

617. 1964 EMMA, Ronald D., *Milton's Grammar,* The Hague, 1964

English poetry, 17C / Milton / Grammar / Parts of speech / Quantitative methods / Syntax

618. 1964 ETIEMBLE, *Parlez-vous Franglais?,* Paris, 1964

French language, 20C / Contrastive studies / Reform, vocabulary / English influence

619. 1964 FLESCH, Rudolf, *The ABC of Style: A Guide To Plain English,* New York, 1964

Usage / Diction / Ars dicendi / Devices / Plain style

620. 1964 FRANCIS, W. Nelson, "A Standard Corpus of Edited Present-Day American English for Computer Use," *Literary Data Processing Conference Proceedings,* ed. Jess B. Bessinger, Stephen M. Parrish and Harry F. Arader, White Plains, N.Y., 1964, pp. 79–89

English language, 20C / American prose, 20C / Vocabulary / Quantitative methods / Computers

621. 1964 GUIRAUD, Pierre, "Le champ stylistique du mot 'ombre' et sa genèse chez Paul Valéry," *Orbis Litterarum,* 1964, pp. 12–26

French poetry, 20C / Valéry / Semantics / Symbol

621a 1964 HAYES, Curtis Wayne, "A Linguistic Analysis of the Prose Style of Edward Gibbon," *Dissertation Abstracts,* XXV (1965), 5268

English prose, 18C / Gibbon / Hemingway / Transformational-generative grammar / Attribution

622. 1964 HONIGFELD, Gilbert, Arthur PLATZ, and Roderic D. GILLIS, "Verbal Style and Personality: Authoritarianism," *Journal of Communication,* XIV (1964), 215–218

Personality / Verbal test / Authoritarian type / Cloze procedure

623. 1964 SAYCE, R., "Quelques réflexions sur le style comique de Molière," *Cahiers de l'association internationale des études françaises,* No. 16 (March 1964), 219–233

French drama, 17C / Molière / Comic style

624. 1964 VOLPE, Edmond L., "Style," *A Reader's Guide to William Faulkner,* New York, 1964, pp. 36–45

American fiction, 20C / Faulkner / Oratory / Speech / Adjectives / Sentence structure

625. 1965 BROOK, Stella, *The Language of the Book of Common Prayer,* London, 1965

English prose, 16C / Biblical prose / Linguistic change / Translation

626. 1965 FRANCE, Peter, *Racine's Rhetoric,* Oxford, 1965

French tragedy, 17C / Racine / Rhetoric, 17C / Tropes / Figures

626a 1965 GREENE, Donald J., " 'Pictures to the Mind': Johnson and Imagery," *Johnson, Boswell and Their Circle: Essays Presented to Lawrence Fitzroy Powell,* ed. Mary Lascelles, *et al.,* Oxford 1965, pp. 137–158

English prose, 18C / Johnson / Imagery / Concreteness / Figurative language

627. 1965 GREGORY, Michael, "Old Bailey Speech in 'A Tale of Two Cities,' " *Review of English Literature,* VI (1965), 42–55

English fiction, 19C / Dickens / Reported speech / Grammar

628. 1965 HILDICK, Wallace, *Word for Word: The Rewriting of Fiction,* New York, 1965

English fiction, 19–20C / Eliot, G. / Lawrence / Butler / Hardy / James / Woolf / Revision

628a 1965 KLEIN, Sheldon, "Control of Style with a Generative Grammar," *Language,* XLI (1965), 619–631

Paraphrasing / Generative grammar / Computers / Sentence generation / Quantitative features

629. 1965 LE HIR, Yves, *Analyses stylistiques,* Paris, 1965

French literature / Explication / Evaluation / Revision / Linguistic history / Corneille / Molière / Racine / Pascal / La Fontaine / Diderot / Bernardin de St. Pierre / Chateaubriand / Baudelaire / Flaubert / Hugo / Verlaine / Loti

630. 1965 LEVINE, George, "The Prose of the *Apologia Pro Vita Sua,*" *Victorian Newsletter,* No. 27 (Spring 1965), 5–8

English prose, 19C / Newman / Concreteness / Diction

631. 1965 MILES, Josephine, "Notes on Prose Style," *Classic Essays in English,* 2d ed., Boston, 1965, pp. xv–xxix

English prose / Historical stylistics / Rhetoric

631a 1965 OHMANN, Richard, "Methods in the Study of Victorian Style," *Victorian Newsletter,* No. 27 (Spring 1965), 1–4

English prose, 19C / Typology / Period style / Generative grammar

632. 1965 ONG, Walter J., "Oral Residue in Tudor Prose Style," *PMLA,* LXXX (1965), 145–154

English prose, 16C / Oral influence / Rhetoric / Genre / Media

633. 1965 SPENCER, John, "A Note on the 'Steady Monologuy of the Interiors'," *Review of English Literature,* VI (1965), 32–41

Reported speech / Linguistics

634. 1965 WRIGHT, Keith, "Rhetorical Repetition in T. S. Eliot's Early Verse," *Review of English Literature,* VI (1965), 93–100

English poetry, 20C / Eliot, T. S. / Rhetoric, Renaissance / Devices / Repetition / Figures

634a 1966 BIARD, Jean Dominique, *The Style of La Fontaine's Fables,* Oxford, 1966

French poetry, 17C / La Fontaine / Vocabulary / Innovation / Colloquialism / Verbs / Word order / Figures

635. 1966 BRIDGMAN, Richard, *The Colloquial Style in America,* New York, 1966

American prose, 19–20C / James, Henry / Twain / Hemingway / Stein, Gertrude / Colloquiality / Concreteness / Syntax / Repetition

636. 1966 CHANDOS, Viscount, *The Well of English Defiled,* London, 1966

English language, 20C / Purism / Decadence

636a 1966 CORBETT, Edward P. J., "A Method of Analyzing Prose Style with a Demonstration Analysis of Swift's 'A Modest Proposal,'" *Reflections on High School English,* ed. Gary Tate, Tulsa, Okla., 1966, pp. 106–124

English prose, 18C / Swift / Diction / Quantitative methods

637. 1966 FRANCIS, Ivor S., "An Exposition of a Statistical Approach to the *Federalist* Dispute," *The Computer and Literary Style,* ed. Jacob Leed, Kent, Ohio, 1966, pp. 38–78

American prose, 18C / Hamilton / Madison / *Federalist* / Quantitative methods: statistical / Computers / Attribution

637a. 1966 GIBSON, Walker, *Tough, Sweet and Stuffy: An Essay on Modern American Prose Styles,* Bloomington, Ind., 1966

Ars dicendi / American prose, 20C / Quantitative methods / Typology

638. 1966 GORDON, Ian A., *The Movement of English Prose,* London, 1966

English prose, history / Development / Diction / Sentence structure / Speech / Social factors

638a 1966 GRAHAM, Victor E., *The Imagery of Proust,* Oxford, 1966

French fiction, 20C / Proust / Thematic imagery / Image-clusters / Quantitative methods

639. 1966 LODGE, David, *Language of Fiction,* London, 1966

English fiction / Theory / Methods / Spitzer / Riffaterre / Linguistics / Translation / Austen / Brontë, C. / Dickens / Hardy / James, Henry / Wells / Amis, Kingsley

640. 1966 MILES, Josephine, and Hanan C. SELVIN, "A Factor Analysis of the Vocabulary of Poetry in the Seventeenth Century," *The Computer and Literary Style,* ed. Jacob Leed, Kent, Ohio, 1966, pp. 116–127

English poetry, 17C / Quantitative methods: factor analysis / Parts of speech / Vocabulary

641. 1966 MILIC, Louis T., "Unconscious Ordering in the Prose of Swift," *The Computer and Literary Style,* ed. Jacob Leed, Kent, Ohio, 1966, pp. 79–106

English prose, 18C / Swift / Quantitative methods / Computers / Parts of speech

641a 1966 MILLER, Henry Knight, "Some Functions of Rhetoric in *Tom Jones,*" *Philological Quarterly,* XLV (1966), 209–235

English fiction, 18C / Fielding / Rhetoric / Rhetorical devices / Figures

642. 1966 MORTON, Andrew Q., and Michael LEVISON, "Some Indications of Authorship in Greek Prose," *The Computer and Literary Style,* ed. Jacob Leed, Kent, Ohio, 1966, pp. 141–179

Greek prose / Attribution / Quantitative methods / Function words / Sentence-length

642a 1966 NILSEN, Don L. F., "Transformation and Development of Style," *English Record,* XVII (Dec. 1966), 38–43

Transformations / Generative grammar / Teaching / Paraphrase

643. 1966 O'DONNELL, Bernard, "Stephen Crane's *The O'Ruddy:* A Problem in Authorship Discrimination," *The Computer and Literary Style,* ed. Jacob Leed, Kent, Ohio, 1966, pp. 107–115

American fiction, 19C / Crane / Attribution / Sentence-length / Word-length / Syntax / Parts of speech

643a 1966 ORAS, Ants, *Blank Verse and Chronology in Milton,* Gainesville, Fla., 1966

English poetry, 17C / Milton / Adjectives / Prosody / Pauses / Word-length / Chronology / Quantitative method

644. 1966 PAGE, Norman, "Standards of Excellence: Jane Austen's Language," *Review of English Literature,* VII (1966), 91–98

English fiction, 19C / Austen / Epithets / Nouns / Adjectives / Diction / Characterization

644a 1966 POIRIER, Richard, *A World Elsewhere: The Place of Style in American Literature,* New York, 1966

American prose, 19–20C / Cooper / Emerson / Hawthorne / James, H. / Melville / Thoreau / Twain / Dreiser / Faulkner / Fitzgerald / Impressionism

644b 1966 RIFFATERRE, Michael, "Describing Poetic Structure: Two Approaches to Baudelaire's *Les Chats,*" *Yale French Studies,* Nos. 36–37 (Oct. 1966), 200–242

French poetry, 19C / Baudelaire / Structure / Poetics

645. 1967 MILIC, Louis T., *A Quantitative Approach to the Style of Jonathan Swift,* The Hague, 1967

English prose, 18C / Swift / Gibbon / Johnson / Addison / Macaulay / Objective methods / Seriation / Connection / Computers / Parts of speech / Attribution

645a 1967 MILLY, J., "Les Pastiches de Proust: Structures et correspondances," *Le français moderne,* XXXV (1967), 33–52

French fiction, 20C / Proust / Parody / Imitation

Part Four

BIBLIOGRAPHIES

A. Separate Bibliographies

646. 1927 KENNEDY, Arthur G., *A Bibliography of Writings on the English Language from the Beginning of Printing to the End of 1922,* New York, 1961, 517 pp.

Topical-chronological, list / History / Pronunciation / Spelling / Etymology / Inflection / Syntax / Semantics / Usage / Rhetoric / Lexicography / Grammar

647. 1949ff. *Linguistic Bibliography for the Year 1939,* "Stylistics," "Mathematical Linguistics," "English," "French," "German," etc., Utrecht, annually

Topical-alphabetical, list / Linguistics / Criticism / Mathematical linguistics

648. 1949ff. *Year's Work in Modern Language Studies,* "Romance Languages: Stylistics" (var. headings), London, annually

Topical, critical / Romance stylistics / Linguistics / Lexicography / Criticism

649. 1953 HATZFELD, Helmut, *A Critical Bibliography of the New Stylistics Applied to the Romance Literatures, 1900–1952,* New York, 1966, 302 pp.

Topical, critical / Romance stylistics / Criticism / Aesthetics / Literature / Theory / Typology / Definition / Survey

650. 1954 GUIRAUD, Pierre, *Bibliographie Critique de la Statistique Linguistique,* Utrecht, 1954, 123 pp.

Topical-chronological, annotated / Mathematical linguistics / Statistics / Phonetics / Metrics / Concordances / Word-counts / Semantics / Morphology / Psycholinguistics

651. 1960 DELAVENAY, E., and K., *Bibliography of Mechanical Translation,* The Hague, 1960, 69 pp.

Topical-alphabetical, annotated / Information theory / Cybernetics / Information retrieval / Abstracting / Computers / Machine translation / Linguistics / Mathematical linguistics

652. 1961 HATZFELD, Helmut, and Yves LE HIR, *Essai de bibliographie critique de stylistique française et romane (1955–1960),* Paris, 1961, 313 pp.

Topical-alphabetical, annotated

653. 1964 CLEARY, James W., and Frederick W. HABERMAN, *Rhetoric and Public Address: A Bibliography, 1947–1961,* Madison and Milwaukee, 1964, 487 pp.

Alphabetical, annotated / Rhetoric / Speech / Oratory / Propaganda / Communication / Preaching

654. 1965 BENNETT, James R., "An Annotated Bibliography of Selected Writings on English Prose Style," *College Composition and Communication,* XVI (1965), 248–255

Topical-alphabetical, annotated

654a 1966 ALLEN, Harold B., *Linguistics and English Linguistics* (Goldentree Bibliographies), New York, 1966

Topical-alphabetical, list

655. 1966 DOHERTY, Paul C., "Stylistics—A Bibliographical Survey," *CEA Critic,* XXVIII (1966), 1, 3–4

Alphabetical, critical

655a 1966 HATZFELD, Helmut A., *A Critical Bibliography of the New Stylistics Applied to the Romance Literatures: 1953–1965,* Chapel Hill, N.C., 1966, 183 pp.

(See also No. 652)

Topical, annotated

B. Bibliographies Included in Other Works

656. 1899 GAYLEY, Charles Mills, and Fred Newton SCOTT, "References," *An Introduction to the Methods and Materials of Literary Criticism,* Boston, 1899, pp. 211–233

Alphabetical, annotated / Criticism / Rhetoric / Language / Literature

656a 1929 LEONARD, Sterling Andrus, "Bibliographies," *The Doctrine of Correctness in English Usage, 1700–1800,* New York, 1962, pp. 309–326

Topical-chronological, annotated / English grammar, 18C / English rhetoric, 18C

657. 1943 WALLACE, Karl R., "Bibliography," *Francis Bacon on Communication and Rhetoric,* Chapel Hill, N.C., 1943, pp. 229–268

Topical-alphabetical, list / Bacon / English rhetorical theory

658. 1948 KAYSER, Wolfgang, "Bibliographie," *Das Sprachliche Kunstwerk,* 5th ed., Berne and Munich, 1959, pp. 391–424

Topical-chronological, list / Prosody / Rhetoric / Syntax / Prose rhythm / Stylistics

659. 1949 WELLEK, René, and Austin WARREN, "Bibliography," *Theory of Literature,* New York, 1949, pp. 347–387

Topical-alphabetical, list / Criticism / Psychology / Sociology / Aesthetics / Prosody / Stylistics / Imagery / Genre

660. 1951 ROSTAND, François, "Bibliographie," *Grammaire et affectivité,* Paris, 1951, pp. 239–261

Topical-alphabetical, list / Grammar / Children's language / Speech disorders

661. 1952 CRADDOCK, Sister Clare Eileen, "Bibliography," *Style Theories as Found in the Stylistic Studies of Romance Scholars, 1900–1950,* Washington, D.C., 1952, pp. 206–212

Topical-alphabetical, list / Romance stylistics

662. 1953 SAYCE, R. A., "Select Bibliography," *Style in French Prose: A Method of Analysis,* Oxford, 1958, pp. 159–161

Topical-chronological, list / French literature

663. 1955 LOCKE, William N., and Andrew Donald BOOTH, "Bibliography," *Machine Translation of Languages,* New Haven and New York, 1955, pp. 227–236

Chronological, annotated / Translation / Machine translation

664. 1957 CHERRY, Colin, "References," *On Human Communication,* Cambridge, Mass. and New York, 1957, pp. 308–323

Alphabetical, list / Information theory / Semantics / Psychology / Communication / Cybernetics / Quantitative methods

665. 1957 ULLMANN, Stephen, "Bibliography," *Style in the French Novel,* Oxford, 1964, pp. 263–269

Topical-alphabetical, list / French novel / Stylistics

666. 1959 FOGARTY, Daniel, "Bibliography," *Roots for a New Rhetoric,* New York, 1959, pp. 141–158

Topical, list / Rhetoric / Composition teaching / New Criticism / General semantics / Burke, K. / Richards, I. A.

667. 1959 MARTIN, Harold C., and Richard M. OHMANN, "A Selective Bibliography," *Style in Prose Fiction,* ed. Harold C. Martin (English Institute Essays, 1958), New York, 1959, pp. 191–200

Alphabetical, list / English and American literature

668. 1959 MORGAN, Bayard Quincy, "A Critical Bibliography of Works on Translation," *On Translation,* ed. Reuben A. Brower, Cambridge, Mass., 1959, pp. 271–293

Chronological, annotated / Translation / Machine translation

669. 1960 LAUSBERG, Heinrich, "Bibliographie," *Handbuch der literarischen Rhetorik,* Munich, 1960, Vol. II, pp. 605–638

Alphabetical, list / Rhetoric, Classical / Literary history / Criticism

670. 1960 SEBEOK, Thomas A., "References," *Style in Language,* Cambridge, Mass. and New York, 1960, pp. 435–449

Alphabetical, list / Linguistics / Criticism / Psycholinguistics / Prosody / Anthropology / Sociology / Information theory

671. 1960 ULLMANN, Stephen, "References," *The Image in the Modern French Novel,* Oxford, 1963, pp. 300–305

Topical-alphabetical, list / Imagery / Modern novel, French / Gide / Proust / Camus / Alain-Fournier

672. 1960 WELLEK, René, "Leo Spitzer (1887–1960)," *Comparative Literature,* XII (1960), 310–344

Topical-chronological, list / Spitzer

673. 1961 POLSKA AKADEMIA NAUK, "References," *Poetics,* Warsaw, 1961, pp. 835–854

Alphabetical, list / Prosody / Metrics / Meaning / Computers / Linguistics / Slavic stylistics

674. 1962 MCLUHAN, Marshall, "Bibliographic Index," *The Gutenberg Galaxy,* Toronto, 1962, pp. 281–289

Alphabetical, list / Communication / Automation

675. 1962 WACKWITZ, Beate, "Literaturverzeichnis," *Die Theorie des Prosastils im England des 18. Jahrhunderts,* Hamburg, 1962, pp. 178–184

Topical-alphabetical, list / English rhetoric, 18C / Ideals, 18C

676. 1963 MINSKY, Marvin, "A Selected Descriptor-Indexed Bibliography to the Literature on Artificial Intelligence," *Computers and Thought,* ed. Edward A. Feigenbaum and Julian Feldman, New York, 1963, pp. 453–523

Alphabetical, descriptive / Computers / Perception / Artificial intelligence / Learning / Brain / Induction / Memory / Information retrieval

677. 1964 GREGORY, Michael, "Bibliography," *Linguistics and Style,* ed. John Spencer, London, 1964, pp. 106–109

Topical-alphabetical, list / Linguistic stylistics

678. 1964 HYMES, Dell H., "General Bibliography," *Language in Culture and Society: A Reader in Linguistics and Anthropology,* New York, 1964, pp. 711–749

Chronological, list / Anthropology / Sociology / Linguistics / Psychology

679. 1965 CORBETT, Edward J. P., "Bibliography," *Classical Rhetoric for the Modern Student,* New York, 1965, pp. 569–574

Topical, list / Rhetoric / Style

680. 1965 DIEBOLD, A. Richard, Jr., "A Survey of Psycholinguistic Research, 1954–1964," *Psycholinguistics,* ed. Charles E. Osgood and Thomas A. Sebeok, Bloomington, Ind., 1965, pp. 205–291

Alphabetical, critical / Psychology / Psycholinguistics / Grammar / Children's language / Semantics / Communication / Information theory

681. 1965 HERTZLER, Joyce O., "Bibliography," *A Sociology of Language,* New York, 1965, pp. 515–548

Topical-alphabetical, list / Sociology / Communication

682. 1965 SHAPIRO, Karl, and Robert BEUM, "A Selected Bibliography," *A Prosody Handbook,* New York, 1965, pp. 203–212

Chronological, list / Prosody / Metrics / Poetics

682a 1966 ERDMAN, David V., and Ephim G. FOGEL, "Annotated Bibliography of Selected Readings," *Evidence for Authorship,* Ithaca, N.Y., 1966, pp. 397–523

Topical, annotated / Attribution / Internal evidence / Forgery / Computers

682b 1966 SCHOENBAUM, S., "Works Cited," *Internal Evidence and Elizabethan Dramatic Authorship,* Evanston, Ill., 1966, pp. 231–256

Alphabetical, list / English drama, 16–17C / Attribution

Part Five

OMNIBUS WORKS

A. Reference

683. 1953 SHIPLEY, Joseph T., *Dictionary of World Literature,* Paterson, N.J., 1960

684. 1960 LAUSBERG, Heinrich, *Handbuch der literarischen Rhetorik,* 2 v., Munich, 1960

685. 1961 MORIER, Henri, *Dictionnaire de poétique et de rhétorique,* Paris, 1961

686. 1965 PREMINGER, Alex, *Encyclopaedia of Poetry and Poetics,* Princeton, 1965

687. 1965 SHAPIRO, Karl, and Robert BEUM, *A Prosody Handbook,* New York, 1965

687a 1966 PEI, Mario, *Glossary of Linguistic Terminology,* New York, 1966

B. Collections

688. 1904 SMITH, G. Gregory, *Elizabethan Critical Essays,* 2 v., Oxford, 1964
Incl., Ascham (13), Puttenham (14)

689. 1905 BREWSTER, William T., *Representative Essays on the Theory of Style,* New York, 1921
Incl., De Quincey (27), Harrison (41), Lewes (32), Newman (31), Pater (38), Spencer (30), Stevenson (37)

690. 1907 COOPER, Lane, *Theories of Style,* New York, 1907
Incl., Aristotle (2), Buffon (19), Coleridge (306), De Quincey (27), Harrison (41), Lewes (32), Longinus (11), Pater (38), Plato (1), Schopenhauer (29), Spencer (30), Stevenson (37)

691. 1908 SPINGARN, J. E., *Critical Essays of the Seventeenth Century,* 3 v., London, 1957
Incl., Jonson (15), Sprat (16)

692. 1915 DURHAM, Willard Higley, *Critical Essays of the Eighteenth Century,* New York, 1961
Incl., Hughes (17)

693. 1928 FULCHER, Paul M., *Foundations of English Style,* New York, 1928

694. 1951 JONES, Richard Foster, *et al., The Seventeenth Century,* Stanford, 1951
Incl., Jones (362, 364, 367), Davis (468)

695. 1955 *Literature and Science* (Proceedings of the Sixth Triennial Congress, International Federation

for Modern Languages and Literatures, 1954), Oxford, 1955
Incl., Barrère (193), Dufrenoy (197), Escarpit (198), Guberina (199), Hatzfeld (200), Vincent (203)

696. 1955 LOCKE, William N., and A. D. BOOTH, *Machine Translation of Languages,* Cambridge, Mass. and New York, 1957
Incl., Bar-Hillel (192), Booth and Locke (194), Bull, Africa and Teichroew (195), Dodd (196), Richens and Booth (202), Weaver (204), Wundheiler (205), Yngve (206)

697. 1958 *Aspects of Translation,* London, 1958
Incl., Booth (214), Forster (216), Tancock (218)

698. 1959 ALLOTT, Miriam, "Style," *Novelists on the Novel,* London, 1959, pp. 308–322

699. 1959 BÖCKMANN, Paul, *Stil- und Formprobleme in der Literatur,* Heidelberg, 1959
Incl., Blackall (533), La Driere (224), Mortier (548), Prescott (552), Tillyard (556), Vergnaud (232), Wilkinson (557)

700. 1959 BROWER, Reuben A., *On Translation,* Cambridge, Mass., 1959
Incl., Brower (534), Fang (538), Fitts (539), Hollander (222), Humphries (542), Jakobson (223), Knight (544), Lattimore (545), Mathews (547), Muir (549), Nabokov (550), Nida (226), O'Brien (551), Oettinger (227), Poggioli (228), Quine (229)

701. 1959 MARTIN, Harold C., *Style in Prose Fiction,* New York, 1959
Incl., Crow (536), Gerber (541), Johnson, S. F. (543), Martin (546), Ohmann (113), Strauss (555)

702. 1960 SEBEOK, Thomas A., *Style in Language,* Cambridge, Mass. and New York, 1960
Incl., Brown and Gilman (561), Carroll (233), Chatman (234), Dorson (565), Hymes (236), Lotz (237), Osgood (238), Saporta (239), Voegelin (241), Wells (242)

703. 1961 BRYANT, Donald C., *The Rhetorical Idiom: Essays in Rhetoric, Oratory, Language, and Drama Presented to Herbert August Wichelns,* Ithaca, N.Y., 1961

704. 1961 HOWES, Raymond F., *Historical Studies of Rhetoric and Rhetoricians,* Ithaca, N.Y., 1961

705. 1961 *Langue et littérature* (Proceedings of the Eighth Congress, International Federation for Modern Languages and Literatures, Liège, 1960), Paris, 1961
Incl., Davis, N. (580), Guiraud (245), Spitzer (250), Ullmann (251)

705a 1961 POLSKA AKADEMIA NAUK, *Poetics,* Warsaw, 1961
Incl., Gorny (119), Masson (120) Skwarczynska (122), Stankiewicz (123), Stutterheim (124), Swieczkowski (586)

706. 1961 SAPORTA, Sol, *Psycholinguistics,* New York, 1961

707. 1961 TUCKER, Susie I., *English Examined,* Cambridge, 1961

708. 1962 BAKER, Carlos, *Ernest Hemingway* (A Scribner Research Anthology), New York, 1962
Incl., Anderson (577), Beach (398), Graham (568), Schorer (405)

709. 1962 GUIRAUD, Pierre *et al., Style et littérature,* The Hague, 1962
Incl., Guiraud (256), Zumthor (130)

710. 1962 HOLMAN, C. Hugh, *Thomas Wolfe* (A Scribner Research Anthology), New York, 1962
Incl., De Voto (461), Frohock (450), Johnson, P. H. (452), Natanson (516), Watkins (522)

711. 1962 *International Conference on Machine Translation of Languages and Applied Language Analysis, 1961,* 2 v., London, 1962

712. 1963 AKHMANOVA, O. S. *et al., Exact Methods in Linguistic Research,* Berkeley and Los Angeles, 1963
Incl., Frumkina (268)

713. 1963 BOURGAUX, Louis, "Le style," *Clarté et prestige de la langue française,* Gembloux, Belgique, 1963, pp. 131–146

714. 1963 CARY, E., and R. W. JUMPELT, *Quality in Translation* (Proceedings of the IIId Congress of the International Federation of Translators, 1959), New York, 1963

715. 1963 GARVIN, Paul L., *Natural Language and the Computer,* New York, 1963

716. 1963 HARDISON, O. B., Jr., *English Literary Criticism: The Renaissance,* New York, 1963
Incl., Ascham (13), Jonson (15), Puttenham (14), Wilson (12)

717. 1964 ARROWSMITH, William, and Roger SHATTUCK, *The Craft and Context of Translation,* New York, 1964

718. 1964 BESSINGER, Jess B., Stephen M. PARRISH, and Harry F. ARADER, *Literary Data Processing Conference Proceedings,* White Plains, N.Y., 1964
Incl., Dearing (616), Fogel (280), Francis, W. N. (620), Markman (283), Raben (287), Sedelow (291)

719. 1964 GARVIN, Paul L., *A Prague School Reader on Esthetics, Literary Structure and Style,* Washington, D.C., 1964

720. 1964 IVES, Sumner, and Stephen O. MITCHELL, *Language, Style, Ideas,* New York, 1964
Incl., Ascham (13), Dobrée (372), Forster (421), Greenburg (528), Ives (269), Jonson (15), Queneau (180), Stevenson (37)

721. 1964 LUNT, Horace G., *Proceedings of the Ninth International Congress of Linguists, Cambridge, Mass., 1962,* The Hague, 1964
Incl., De Groot (278), Halliday (281), Levin, S. R. (139), Riffaterre (140), Winter (142)

722. 1964 WERMUTH, Paul C., *Modern Essays on Writing and Style,* New York, 1964
Incl., Connolly (384), Dobrée (372), Graves and Hodge (422), Lucas (101), Montague (63), Murry (53), Orwell (441), Raleigh (40), Read (62), Rouse (404), Sapir (51), Smith, L. P. (378)

723. 1965 BAILEY, Dudley, *Essays on Rhetoric,* New York, 1965
Incl., Aristotle (2), Blair (23), Campbell (21), Cicero (5), Joos (259), Plato (1), Quintilian (10), Spencer, H. (30)

723a 1965 KREUZER, Helmut, and Rul GUNZENHAUSER, *Mathematik und Dichtung,* Munich, 1965

724\. 1965 SCHWARTZ, Joseph, and John A. RYCENGA, *The Province of Rhetoric,* New York, 1965
Incl., Baldwin (59), Beaumont (578), Crane (382), Fogarty (111), Howell (439), McKeon (74), Tuve (447), Weaver (99)

725\. 1966 BOLTON, W. F., *The English Language: Essays by English and American Men of Letters, 1490–1839,* Cambridge, 1966

725a 1966 CUNNINGHAM, J. V., *The Problem of Style,* New York, 1966

725b 1966 ERDMAN, David V., and Ephim G. FOGEL, *Evidence for Authorship,* Ithaca, N.Y., 1966
Incl., Lord (529), Sherbo (231)

726\. 1966 FOWLER, Roger, *Essays in Language and Style,* London, 1966

727\. 1966 LEED, Jacob, *The Computer and Literary Style,* Kent, Ohio, 1966
Incl., Francis, Ivor (637), Miles and Selvin (640), Milic (641), Morton and Levison (642), O'Donnell (643), Sedelow (290), Somers (299), Wachal (300)

728\. 1966 SMITH, Alfred G., *Communication and Culture,* New York, 1966

729\. 1966 WATKINS, Floyd C., and Karl F. KNIGHT, *Writer to Writer: Readings on the Craft of Writing,* Boston, 1966

730\. 1967 CHATMAN, Seymour, and S. R. LEVIN, *Essays in the Language of Literature,* Boston, 1967
Incl., Beardsley (108), Brooke-Rose (525), Chatman (234), Halliday (281), Levin, S. R. (139), Miles (272),

(Continued)

Milic (158), Ohmann (113), Riffaterre (114, 118), Wimsatt (407)

730a 1967 STEINMANN, Martin, Jr., *New Rhetorics*, New York, 1967
Incl., Beardsley (152a), Milic (298), Ohmann (285)

Index 1

AUTHORS AS CONTRIBUTORS

Index 2

AUTHORS AS SUBJECTS

Index 3

SUBJECTS AND TOPICS

Appendix

The following items include: (a) works that appeared too late for inclusion in the main body of the Bibliography; (b) works of earlier date which on a review of the literature were considered of sufficient importance to deserve inclusion. The items are given the numbers that would have been assigned to them above, arranged in numerical order, and grouped according to the parts in which they would have been placed. None of these items is included in the Indexes.

I: THEORETICAL

153a 1966 CHATMAN, Seymour, "On the Theory of Literary Style," *Linguistics,* No. 27 (Nov. 1966), 13–25

Definition / Connotation / Style as Meaning / Purport / Choice /Idiosyncratic style

157a 1966 WEATHERS, Winston, "The Rhetoric of the Series," *College Composition and Communication,* XVII (1966), 217–222

◈ Repr., *Teaching Freshman Composition,* ed. Gary Tate and Edward P. J. Corbett, New York, 1967, pp. 313–319

Rhetorical devices / Seriation / Impressionistic method

157b 1967 CHATMAN, Seymour, "'Style': A Narrow View," *College Composition and Communication,* XVIII (1967), 72–76

Definition / Meaning / Grammar

158c 1967 POSNER, Rebecca, "Positivism in Historical Linguistics," *Romance Philology,* XX (1967), 321–331 (Rev. of No. 132)

II: METHODOLOGICAL

297d 1966 ELLIS, Allan B., and André FAVAT, "From Computer to Criticism: An Application of Automatic Content Analysis to the Study of Literature," *The General Inquirer,* ed. Philip J. Stone *et al.,* Cambridge, Mass., 1966, pp. 628–638

Content analysis / General Inquirer / Computers / American fiction, 19C / Twain

297e 1966 HAYES, Curtis W., "A Study in Prose Styles: Edward Gibbon and Ernest Hemingway," *Texas Studies in Literature and Language,* VII (1966), 371–386

Generative-transformational grammar / Syntax / Statistical methods / Gibbon / Hemingway

300b 1967 KROEBER, Karl, "Computers and Research in Literary Analysis," *Computers in Humanistic Research,* ed. Edmund A. Bowles, Englewood Cliffs, N.J., 1967, pp. 135–142

Computers / Quantitative methods / Parts of speech / Syntax / English fiction, 19C / Austen, J. / Eliot, G. / Brontë, C. and E.

III: APPLIED

356a 1928 RYLANDS, George H. W., *Words and Poetry,* London, 1928

English drama, 16–17C / Shakespeare / Diction / Adjectives / Latinism / Saxonism / Symbolism

375a 1935 THOMPSON, Elbert N. S., "Milton's Prose Style," *Philological Quarterly,* XIV (1935), 1–15

English prose, 17C / Milton / Sentence structure / Word order / Latinism / Diction

455a 1949 ARTHOS, John, *The Language of Natural Description in Eighteenth-Century Poetry,* New York, 1966

English poetry, 18C / Stock diction / Natural history / Scientific style / Periphrasis / Epithets

456a 1949 EKFELT, Fred Emil, "Latinate Diction in Milton's English Prose," *Philological Quarterly,* XXVIII (1949), 53–71

English prose, 17C / Milton / Diction / Latinism

506a 1956 CLARK, Evert Mordecai, "Milton's English Poetical Vocabulary," *Studies in Philology,* LIII (1956), 220–238

English poetry, 17C / Milton / Vocabulary size / Romance-Saxon / Quantitative methods

513a 1957 HATZFELD, Helmut, *Trends and Styles in Twentieth-Century Literature,* 2d ed., Washington, D.C., 1966

French literature, 20C / Contemporary style / Typology / Imagery / Reflection theory

524a 1958 BROADBENT, J. B., "Milton's Rhetoric," *Modern Philology,* LVI (1958), 224–242

(Continued)

English poetry, 17C / Milton / Rhetorical figures

632a 1965 SALMON, Vivian, "Sentence Structures in Colloquial Shakespearian English," *Transactions of the Philological Society, 1965,* Oxford, 1966, pp. 105–140

English drama, 16C / Shakespeare / Colloquial speech / Syntax / Sentence types / Stimulus-response principle

633a 1965 WRIGHT, Andrew, "Language and Play," *Henry Fielding: Mask and Feast,* Berkeley and Los Angeles, 1966, pp. 172–191

English fiction, 18C / Fielding / Ideals / Plain style / Grand style / Figurative language / Jargon / Multiple styles

644c 1967 BICKERTON, Derek, "The Language of *Women in Love,*" *Review of English Literature,* VIII (Apr. 1967), 56–67

English fiction, 20C / Lawrence, D. H. / Bad style / Inflation / Repetition / Modification

644d 1967 BURKE, Phyllis Brown, "Rhetorical Considerations of Bacon's 'Style'," *College Composition and Communication,* XVIII (1967), 23–31

English prose, 16–17C / Bacon / Alteration / Revision / Analogy / Proverb / Argument / Audience

644e 1967 FROHOCK, W. M., *Style and Temper: Studies in French Fiction, 1925–1960,* Oxford, 1967

French fiction, 20C / Montherlant / Saint-Exupêry / Bernanos / Malraux / Imagery / Levels / Coherence / Duration

644f 1967 MILES, Josephine, *Style and Proportion: The Language of Prose and Poetry,* Boston, 1967

English language / Stylistic devices / Historical survey / Word-frequency / Keywords / Quantitative methods / Rhythm / Metrics / Nouns / Adjectives / Verbs

645b 1967 STEDMOND, John M., "The Question of Style," *The Comic Art of Laurence Sterne,* Toronto, 1967, pp. 30–47
(*See* No. 554)

English fiction, 18C / Sterne / Conversational style / Stylistic devices / Innovation / Convention

IV: BIBLIOGRAPHIES

B. Bibliographies Included in Other Works

682c 1967 MILES, Josephine, "Works on Style," *Style and Proportion,* Boston, 1967, pp. 164–212

Alphabetical, list / General

V: OMNIBUS WORKS

B. Collections

730b 1967 CHRISTENSEN, Francis, *Notes Toward a New Rhetoric,* New York, 1967

Incl. Christensen (267, 604)

730c 1967 GORRELL, Robert M., *Rhetoric: Theories for Application,* Champaign, Ill., 1967

730d 1967 TATE, Gary, and Edward P. J. CORBETT, *Teaching Freshman Composition,* New York, 1967

Incl. Bennett (654), Corbett (636a), Doherty (655),) Milic (146), Ohmann (285), Weathers (157a)